THE PRATYUTPANNA
SAMĀDHI SUTRA

THE ŚŪRAṄGAMA
SAMĀDHI SUTRA

BDK English Tripiṭaka 25-II, 25-III

The Pratyutpanna Samādhi Sutra

Translated by

Lokakṣema

Translated from the Chinese

(Taishō Volume 13, Number 418)

by

Paul Harrison

The Śūraṅgama Samādhi Sutra

Translated by

Kumārajīva

Translated from the Chinese

(Taishō Volume 15, Number 642)

by

John McRae

Numata Center
for Buddhist Translation and Research
1998

First Printing, 1998
ISBN: 1-886439-06-0
Library of Congress Catalog Card Number: 97-069169

Published by
Numata Center for Buddhist Translation and Research
2620 Warring Street
Berkeley, California 94704

Printed in the United States of America

A Message on the Publication of the English Tripiṭaka

The Buddhist canon is said to contain eighty-four thousand different teachings. I believe that this is because the Buddha's basic approach was to prescribe a different treatment for every spiritual ailment, much as a doctor prescribes a different medicine for every medical ailment. Thus his teachings were always appropriate for the particular suffering individual and for the time at which the teaching was given, and over the ages not one of his prescriptions has failed to relieve the suffering to which it was addressed.

Ever since the Buddha's Great Demise over twenty-five hundred years ago, his message of wisdom and compassion has spread throughout the world. Yet no one has ever attempted to translate the entire Buddhist canon into English throughout the history of Japan. It is my greatest wish to see this done and to make the translations available to the many English-speaking people who have never had the opportunity to learn about the Buddha's teachings.

Of course, it would be impossible to translate all of the Buddha's eighty-four thousand teachings in a few years. I have, therefore, had one hundred thirty-nine of the scriptural texts in the prodigious Taishō edition of the Chinese Buddhist canon selected for inclusion in the First Series of this translation project.

It is in the nature of this undertaking that the results are bound to be criticized. Nonetheless, I am convinced that unless someone takes it upon himself or herself to initiate this project, it will never be done. At the same time, I hope that an improved, revised edition will appear in the future.

It is most gratifying that, thanks to the efforts of more than a hundred Buddhist scholars from the East and the West, this monumental project has finally gotten off the ground. May the rays of the Wisdom of the Compassionate One reach each and every person in the world.

NUMATA Yehan
Founder of the English
Tripiṭaka Project

August 7, 1991

Editorial Foreword

In January, 1982, Dr. NUMATA Yehan, the founder of the Bukkyō Dendō Kyōkai (Society for the Promotion of Buddhism), decided to begin the monumental task of translating the complete Taishō edition of the Chinese Tripiṭaka (Buddhist Canon) into the English language. Under his leadership, a special preparatory committee was organized in April, 1982. By July of the same year, the Translation Committee of the English Tripiṭaka was officially convened.

The initial Committee consisted of the following members: HANAYAMA Shōyū (Chairperson); BANDŌ Shōjun; ISHIGAMI Zennō; KAMATA Shigeo; KANAOKA Shūyū; MAYEDA Sengaku; NARA Yasuaki; SAYEKI Shinkō; (late) SHIOIRI Ryōtatsu; TAMARU Noriyoshi; (late) TAMURA Kwansei; URYŪZU Ryūshin; and YUYAMA Akira. Assistant members of the Committee were as follows: KANAZAWA Atsushi; WATANABE Shōgo; Rolf Giebel of New Zealand; and Rudy Smet of Belgium.

After holding planning meetings on a monthly basis, the Committee selected 139 texts for the First Series of translations, an estimated one hundred printed volumes in all. The texts selected are not necessarily limited to those originally written in India but also include works written or composed in China and Japan. While the publication of the First Series proceeds, the texts for the Second Series will be selected from among the remaining works; this process will continue until all the texts, in Japanese as well as in Chinese, have been published.

Frankly speaking, it will take perhaps one hundred years or more to accomplish the English translation of the complete Chinese and Japanese texts, for they consist of thousands of works. Nevertheless, as Dr. NUMATA wished, it is the sincere hope of the Committee that this project will continue unto completion, even after all its present members have passed away.

It must be mentioned here that the final object of this project is not academic fulfillment but the transmission of the teaching of the

Buddha to the whole world in order to create harmony and peace among mankind. Therefore, although scholarly notes are indispensable for academic purposes, they are not given in the English translations because they might distract the general reader's attention from the valuable content of the Buddhist scriptures. Instead, simple endnotes and a glossary are added at the end of each work, in accordance with the respective translators' wish.

To my great regret, however, Dr. NUMATA passed away on May 5, 1994, at the age of 97, entrusting his son, Mr. NUMATA Toshihide, with the continuation and completion of the Translation Project. The Committee also lost its able and devoted Chairperson, Professor HANAYAMA Shōyū, on June 16, 1995, at the age of 63. After these severe blows, the Committee elected me, Vice-President of the Musashino Women's College, to be the Chair in October, 1995. The Committee has renewed its determination to carry out the noble intention of Dr. NUMATA, under the leadership of Mr. NUMATA Toshihide.

The present members of the Committee are MAYEDA Sengaku (Chairperson), BANDŌ Shōjun, ISHIGAMI Zennō, ICHISHIMA Shōshin, KAMATA Shigeo, KANAOKA Shūyū, NARA Yasuaki, SAYEKI Shinkō, TAMARU Noriyoshi, URYŪZU Ryūshin, and YUYAMA Akira. Assistant members are WATANABE Shōgo and MINOWA Kenryō.

The Numata Center for Buddhist Translation and Research was established in November, 1984, in Berkeley, California, U.S.A., to assist in the publication of the BDK English Tripiṭaka First Series. In December, 1991, the Publication Committee was organized at the Numata Center, with Professor Philip Yampolsky as the Chairperson. To our sorrow, Professor Yampolsky passed away in July, 1996, but thankfully Dr. Kenneth Inada is continuing the work as Chairperson. The Numata Center has thus far published eleven volumes and has been distributing them. All of the remaining texts will be published under the supervision of this Committee, in close cooperation with the Translation Committee in Tokyo.

MAYEDA Sengaku
Chairperson
Translation Committee of
the BDK English Tripiṭaka

June 1, 1997

Publisher's Foreword

The Publication Committee works in close cooperation with the Editorial Committee of the BDK English Tripiṭaka in Tokyo, Japan. Since December 1991, it has operated from the Numata Center for Buddhist Translation and Research in Berkeley, California. Its principal mission is to oversee and facilitate the publication in English of selected texts from the one hundred-volume Taishō Edition of the Chinese Tripiṭaka, along with a few major influential Japanese Buddhist texts not in the Tripiṭaka. The list of selected texts is conveniently appended at the end of each volume. In the text itself, the Taishō Edition page and column designations are provided in the margins.

The Committee is committed to the task of publishing clear, readable English texts. It honors the deep faith, spirit, and concern of the late Reverend Doctor NUMATA Yehan to disseminate Buddhist teachings throughout the world.

In July 1996, the Committee unfortunately lost its valued Chairperson, Dr. Philip Yampolsky, who was a stalwart leader, trusted friend, and esteemed colleague. We follow in his shadow. In February 1997, I was appointed to guide the Committee in his place.

The Committee is charged with the normal duties of a publishing firm—general editing, formatting, copyediting, proofreading, indexing, and checking linguistic fidelity. The Committee members are Diane Ames, Brian Galloway, Nobuo Haneda, Charles Niimi, Koh Nishiike, and the president and director of the Numata Center, Reverend Kiyoshi S. Yamashita.

Kenneth K. Inada
Chairperson,
Publication Committee

June 1, 1997

Contents

BDK English Tripiṭaka 25-II

The Pratyutpanna Samādhi Sutra

Translated by

Lokakṣema

Translated from the Chinese

(Taishō Volume 13, Number 418)

by

Paul Harrison

Numata Center
for Buddhist Translation and Research
1998

Contents

Translator's Introduction

No one could claim that the *Banzhou-sanmei-jing,* Lokakṣema's pioneering translation of the *Pratyutpanna-buddha-saṃmukhāvasthita-samādhi-sūtra,* is one of the great works of Chinese literature, but its historical significance is beyond dispute. The Indo-Scythian Lokakṣema, active as a translator in the Later Han capital of Luoyang during the years 170–190 C.E., is credited with the introduction of Mahayana Buddhism into China. The *Pratyutpanna-buddha-saṃmukhāvasthita-samādhi-sūtra* (hereafter abbreviated to *PraS*) was one of the first Mahayana scriptures he translated into Chinese; in the absence of any other data, this makes the *Banzhou-sanmei-jing* the oldest documentary evidence relating to that movement for which a precise date can be established. It shares this honor with the *Aṣṭa-sāhasrikā-prajñā-pāramitā-sūtra* (*Perfection of Wisdom in Eight Thousand Lines*): according to contemporary colophons, the two sutras were translated in the same year, 179 C.E. They are thus important sources of information on the early development of Mahayana Buddhism, even though it may not be appropriate to regard them as early Mahayana sutras themselves.

The year 179 C.E. is, of course, merely the date of the translation; it does not tell us when the *PraS* was first composed. This could have been in the first half of the second century C.E., the first century, or even earlier. Internal evidence, however, suggests that the text appeared some five hundred years after the death of Gautama. That date too is a matter of some controversy, but whether we accept the current 'best guess' (circa 486 B.C.E.) or put the Parinirvāṇa closer to the year 400, to place the composition of the *PraS* sometime in the first century C.E. may not be too wide of the mark. Although its exact date is likely to remain uncertain, the *PraS* clearly demonstrates that even in what we might call its Early Middle Period, i.e. by the second century C.E., the Mahayana was a heterogeneous movement embracing several different strains and tendencies. What makes the *PraS* historically interesting is its attempt to reconcile and harmonize some of these tendencies.

The *PraS* is generally thought to be a work of Pure Land Buddhism. Certainly it has been much used by followers of that school in China and Japan, as well as by adherents of other sects. The great Chinese monk Huiyuan (334–416), founder of the White Lotus Society dedicated to the worship of Amitābha and to rebirth in the paradise of Sukhāvatī, was well-acquainted with the text, as his correspondence with Kumārajīva (344–413) shows. Other Buddhist thinkers who cited the *PraS* in their writings include such luminaries as the Tiantai patriarch Zhiyi (538–97), Daochuo (562–645), Shan-dao (613–81), and Jiacai (fl. c. 627–49) on the Chinese side, and Genshin (942–1017) and Hōnen (1133–1212) in Japan, where the *PraS* is still regarded as an important text by various branches of the Jōdo Sect. However, to call the *PraS* a Pure Land sutra is a radical oversimplification, for it is certainly not at all like the other great sutras of that school, the larger and smaller *Sukhāvatī-vyūha-sūtra*s and the so-called *Amitāyur-dhyāna-sūtra*. Whereas these texts glorify the compassionate action of the former bodhisattva Dharmākara and show the faithful the way to rebirth in Sukhāvatī, the glorious Buddha-field of the Buddha Amitābha/Amitāyus, the *PraS* follows a different agenda. As its name indicates, it propounds a particular samādhi, or meditation, called the *pratyutpanna-buddha-saṃmukhāvasthita-samādhi,* i.e. "the meditation in which one is brought face to face with the Buddhas of the present" or "the meditation of direct encounter with the Buddhas of the present." This meditation is a developed form of the earlier practice of *buddhānusmṛti,* or "calling the Buddha to mind" (Chinese *nianfo;* Japanese *nembutsu*). The object of this "calling to mind" or visualization may accordingly be all or any of the myriad Buddhas of the present, and although the text of the *PraS* mentions Amitābha by name, he is merely adduced as an example, as the Buddha of the present *par excellence*. The practitioner of the meditation might just as well visualize the Buddha of the east, Akṣobhya, in his Buddha-field Abhirati. If, therefore, Pure Land Buddhism is understood as relating only to Amitābha and Sukhāvatī, then the *PraS* was not originally a Pure Land text as such, even though it deals with many key features of Pure Land belief and practice.

Another distinguishing feature of the *PraS* is its attempt to reconcile the vision of the Buddhas and Buddha-fields of the present (and the goal of rebirth in them) with the insights of the Perfection of Wisdom school, by which we mean the Śūnyavāda (theory of emptiness) tendency in Mahayana Buddhism. The three main Pure Land texts mentioned above approach their subject with a certain "realism": Amitābha and Sukhāvatī are presented to all intents and purposes as if they actually exist. But the *PraS* is scrupulous about setting the experiences of the meditator against the yardstick of *śūnyatā*, or "emptiness", so that no attachment arises. The visions of the Buddhas of the present and the accompanying hearing of the Dharma which they proclaim are, however, no mere hallucinations: they are valid perceptions, but they are "empty" at the same time. This is the central paradox of the *PraS*, the resolution of which depends not on intellectualization but on the proper use of the faculty of wisdom, on meditational development, and on moral self-cultivation, this last being a subject on which the *PraS* has a great deal to say. All this is very much in the style of the Perfection of Wisdom sutras, which provided the basis for the Madhyamaka school of Mahayana Buddhism. At the same time, it foreshadows one of the fundamental principles of the "deity yoga" regarded as typical of Vajrayāna or Tantric Buddhism.

The *PraS* also contains hints of the early unfolding of the Yogācāra ("Practice of Yoga") school, the most striking of which is the phrase (in Chap. II of the *Banzhou-sanmei-jing*) "These Three Realms are simply made by thought," which reappears in the *Daśabhūmika-sūtra* in its Sanskrit form: *cittamātram idam yad idaṃ traidhātukam*. As its name suggests, the Yogācāra school (also known as Cittamātra or "Thought-Only") drew its inspiration from a process of creative generalization, in which the insights derived from meditational practice (*yoga*) were applied to all experience. The *PraS* contains many examples of this creative generalization, the most dramatic of which are drawn from the realm of dreams.

The *PraS,* therefore, incorporates elements of all the major tendencies within the Buddhist movement known as the Mahayana. What is more, it contrives to weave them into a harmonious pattern. In the process it draws in much other fascinating material, but it is this creative synthesis which gives the work its primary historical significance.

It remains to be asked whether this Mahayana sutra, significant though it may be, is well served by Lokakṣema's translation of it. However, this question does not admit of an easy answer, since, save for one small fragment, the original Sanskrit text of the *PraS* has been lost. The most reliable translation we have left is undoubtedly the Tibetan, the *'Phags-pa da-ltar-gyi sangs-rgyas mngon-sum-du bzhugs-pa'i ting-nge-'dzin ces-bya-ba theg-pa-chen-po'i mdo,* produced at the beginning of the ninth century by Śākyaprabha and Ratnarakṣita. Although it represents a later form of the text, it is indispensable for elucidating obscurities in the Chinese translations, of which four survive (Nos. 416–19 in Vol. XIII of the *Taishō shinshū daizōkyō*). When we come to look at these Chinese versions, however, we enter a minefield of text-historical problems, and only the most careful and painstaking research will enable us to pick our way through it. Little more than a bare summary of our conclusions can be presented here. First of all, the *Banzhou-sanmei-jing* in three volumes (*juan*), which is now ascribed to Lokakṣema, exists in two separate redactions. Redaction A appears in the Tripiṭaka Koreana, and was taken as the base text for the *Taishō* edition (No. 418). With a number of essential emendations, it is the text which is translated here. Redaction B appears in the Song, Yuan, and Ming printings of the Chinese Canon, and its readings are given in the footnotes to the Taishō edition. Redactions A and B differ substantially only up to halfway through Chapter IV (the end of Chapter VI in the Tibetan version); after that point they are basically the same text. In other words, Redaction A proper, which is distinguished primarily by its prose translations of

Sanskrit verses, is partial, comprising somewhat less than the first third of the text. It is only Redaction A which can be ascribed unreservedly to Lokakṣema; Redaction B is, in part at least, the work of a later hand, a revision of the translation most probably carried out by one of Lokakṣema's disciples in the year 208, entailing, among other things, a retranslation of the Sanskrit verses into Chinese verse. It is possible that Lokakṣema himself had only the first third of the sutra at his disposal, and that the enlarged Sanskrit text was brought to China soon after 179 C.E. This supposition is given added weight by the existence of an incomplete Chinese version of the *PraS*, the *Bapo-pusa-jing* (*Taishō* 419), which must have appeared by the middle of the third century. The *Bapo-pusa-jing* also ends abruptly at the same point as that at which Redaction A of the *Banzhou-sanmei-jing* merges with Redaction B. All this might lead us to hypothesize a shorter *Urtext* of the *PraS*, were it not for the fact that all the prose passages of our Redaction B bear the stamp of Lokakṣema's style. Next we ought to account for *Taishō* 417, the *Banzhou-sanmei-jing* in one volume, which is also ascribed to Lokakṣema, and which has been accorded such a high place in Japan. Despite all assertions to the contrary, it is in fact not an independent translation of the *PraS* at all, but merely an abridged pastiche of Redaction B of the *Banzhou-sanmei-jing* in three volumes. Finally, the least problematical of the Chinese versions of the *PraS* is *Taishō* 416, the *Dafangdeng-daji-jing-xianhu-fen* (i.e. the "Bhadrapāla Section" of the *Mahāvaipulya-mahāsaṃnipāta-sūtra*) in five volumes, produced by Jñānagupta *et al.* in 595 C.E. The text differs in certain respects from that translated by Lokakṣema, and it is also interesting to note that by this time the *PraS* was regarded as part of the massive compendium of Mahayana sutras known as the *Mahāsaṃnipāta*. In conclusion, then, the *Banzhou-sanmei-jing* which has here been translated into English is only partly the work of Lokakṣema himself, but since the rest of the text may fairly be ascribed to the *school* of Lokakṣema, it is not out of place to let the traditional attribution stand.

As previously noted, Lokakṣema pioneered the translation of Mahayana sutras in China. He was working in largely uncharted territory, and may not have been very fluent in Chinese, while his Chinese assistants, for their part, would have been quite unfamiliar with the conceptual content and the idiom of the literature they were helping to translate. To get his message across, Lokakṣema frequently cut the text down, almost to the bone. Despite this, the version of the *PraS* which he and his assistants produced is often disjointed and crude, and fairly bristles with obscure or unintelligible passages, defects which can only have been exacerbated by centuries of scribal transmission. The present English translation does the best it can with these problem passages, at the same time making no attempt to gloss over the infelicities of the archaic Buddhist Chinese which makes Lokakṣema's works so valuable a resource for Chinese historical linguistics. It also endeavors to convey the inventiveness displayed by Lokakṣema in rendering Buddhist terminology in Chinese (although his frequent transcriptions of Sanskrit words have mostly been translated into English); this is especially apparent in his use of Taoist vocabulary, e.g. "the Way" (*Tao*) for "awakening" (*bodhi*), "non-action" (*wuwei*) for nirvana, and "original non-being" (*benwu*) for "suchness" (*tathatā*). In this way, it is hoped, this translation remains true to the spirit of Lokakṣema's work, and the *Banzhou-sanmei-jing* in three volumes stands revealed as the magnificent achievement in cross-cultural communication that it was.

Paul Harrison

Fascicle One

Chapter I

Questions

The Buddha was at the Haunt of the Squirrels in the Great Wood at Rājagṛha with a great assembly of monks consisting of five hundred men, all of whom had attained arhatship, with the sole exception of Ānanda. At that time a certain bodhisattva by the name of Bhadrapāla, together with five hundred bodhisattvas, all of whom kept the five precepts, arrived in the late afternoon at the place where the Buddha was, and, having come forward and 903a
touched the Buddha's feet with his forehead, withdrew and sat down to one side. With him also were five hundred ascetics, who arrived at the place where the Buddha was, and, having come forward and made obeisance to the Buddha, withdrew and sat down to one side.

Then the Buddha displayed his numinous power, so that all monks would come from wherever they happened to be, and straightaway one hundred thousand monks came, one after another, and assembled at the place where the Buddha was. Having come forward and made obeisance to the Buddha, they withdrew and sat down to one side. Once again the Buddha displayed his numinous power, so that the nun Mahāprajāpatī, together with thirty thousand nuns, arrived, one after the other, at the place where the Buddha was, and, having come forward and made obeisance to the Buddha, they withdrew and sat down to one side.

Once again the Buddha displayed his numinous power, so that the bodhisattva Ratnākara left the great city of Vaiśālī, the bodhisattva Guhagupta left the great city of Campā, the bodhisattva Naradatta left the great city of Vārāṇasī, the bodhisattva Susīma left the great city of Kapilavastu, the bodhisattva Mahāsuārthavāha together with the householder Anāthapiṇḍada left the great city of Śrāvastī, the bodhisattva Indradatta left the great city of Kauśāmbī, and the bodhisattva Varuṇadeva left the great city of Sāketa. Each of these bodhisattvas, accompanied by twenty-eight thousand people, came to where the Buddha was, and having come forward and made obeisance to the Buddha, they all withdrew and sat down to one side. King Ajātaśatru of Rājagṛha, together with one hundred thousand people, came to where the Buddha was, and having come forward and made obeisance to the Buddha, they withdrew and sat down to one side. The Four Heavenly Kings, Śakra, Lord of the Gods, Brahmā Sahāṃpati, the god Maheśvara and the Akaniṣṭha gods, each accompanied by many million million hundred thousand[1] sons of gods, came to where the Buddha was, and having come forward and made obeisance to the Buddha, they withdrew and took up a position to one side. The dragon kings Nanda and Upananda, the dragon king Sāgara, the dragon king Manasvin and the dragon king Anavatapta, each accompanied by many million million hundred thousand myriad dragon kings, came to where the Buddha was, and having come forward and made obeisance to the Buddha, they withdrew and took up a position to one side. The Asura kings of the four quarters, each accompanied by many million million hundred thousand myriad Asura people, came to where the Buddha was, and having come forward and made obeisance to the Buddha, they withdrew and took up a position to one side. By this time the monks and the nuns, the laymen and the laywomen, the gods, the dragons, the Asura people, the Yakṣa spirits, the Garuḍa spirits, the Kinnara spirits, the Mahoraga spirits, the humans and the nonhumans were past counting and beyond all reckoning.

The bodhisattva Bhadrapāla rose from his seat, put his robes in order, placed his hands together with interlacing fingers, went

down on his knees, and said to the Buddha: "I wish to ask a question, and when I have asked it I should like to have the matter resolved. If the God among Gods will allow me to speak, I shall now question the Buddha." The Buddha said to the bodhisattva Bhadra- 903b
pāla: "Ask right away about those matters which are to be resolved, and the Buddha will explain them to you."

The bodhisattva Bhadrapāla asked the Buddha: "What kind of meditation ought bodhisattvas to practise so that: the wisdom they attain is like the ocean, or like Mount Sumeru; they do not doubt what they hear; they never fail to be those among men who are going to achieve the attainment of Buddhahood for themselves, without ever turning back; they are never born among the stupid; they know what is past and anticipate what is to come; they are never parted from the Buddhas, and are not parted from them even in their dreams; they are upright and handsome, and among the masses the fineness of their features is without compare; as children they are always born into great and noble families; they are respected and loved by all their parents, brothers, relatives and friends; they are highly talented and have wide learning; they acquit themselves in debate quite differently from the masses; they keep themselves under control; they always feel a sense of shame; they are never conceited; they are always loving and compassionate; their insight is penetrating; among the wise there is none to equal them in understanding; they have an incomparable numinous presence; their energy is hard to match; they immerse themselves in the sutras; they constantly immerse themselves in the sutras; they understand everything in the sutras; they take pleasure in immersing themselves in states of trance and concentration; they immerse themselves in emptiness, formlessness, and nonattachment, and feel no fear with regard to these three things; they frequently preach the sutras to others, and they keep them safe as they deem fit; wherever they wish to be born, they get what they want and nothing else; the power of their merit and the power of their faith are considerable; wherever they go, their physical powers are strong; they all [have] the power of love; they all

have the power of the bases [i.e. the senses]; they are brilliant in [their understanding and use of] the power of the objects [of the senses]; they are brilliant in the power of thought; they are brilliant in the power of visualization; they are brilliant in the power of faith; they are brilliant in the power of vows; they are like the ocean in their learning in that it is forever inexhaustible; they are like the moon when it is full in that they shine everywhere; in that there is nothing that is not touched by their light, they are like the sun when it rises; they are like a torch, in that where they shine there are no obstructions; they are unattached, their minds being like empty space in that they do not settle anywhere; they are like adamant, in that they can penetrate anything; they are stable like Mount Meru, in that they cannot be moved; they are like the threshold of a gate in that they remain steadfast and true; their minds are soft like goosedown, in that there is no roughness in them; they renounce their personal interests, and are free of longing; they take pleasure in mountains and streams, like wild beasts; they always keep themselves to themselves, and do not have intercourse with others; as to ascetics and men of the Way, they are frequently instructed by them and look after them all; if people treat them with contempt or molest them, they never harbor angry thoughts; all the Māras cannot move them; they understand the sutras and immerse themselves in the various kinds of wisdom; they study all the Buddha-dharmas, and nobody [else] can act as teacher to them; their authority and sageliness are unshakeable; their conduct, which is deeply absorbed, always con-
903c forms to nonbeing; their conduct is always gentle and they are always moved to pity by the sutras; they serve the Buddhas untiringly; their conduct is diverse, and they attain all meritorious virtues; their conduct is always perfectly truthful; their faith is always correct, and cannot be disturbed; their conduct is always pure, and in a crisis they can act resolutely without difficulty; they are pure in their wisdom, which understands all; they attain pleasurable conduct; they eliminate the five obscurations; in knowledge and conduct they gradually work their way towards the realm of Buddhahood, adorning all

lands; in moral discipline they are pure of the thoughts of arhats and pratyekabuddhas; they carry to completion everything they do; in acting meritoriously they always take the lead and they teach the people to do likewise; they do not weary of what is taught among bodhisattvas, and in their conduct their transcendence is unbounded among all [adherents of] other ways; there is none who can touch them; they are never separated from the Buddha, or fail to see the Buddha; they always think of the Buddhas as being no different from their parents; gradually they attain the numinous power of the Buddhas and acquire the light of all the sutras; their vision is unobstructed, and all the Buddhas stand before them; they are like magicians, masters of the dharmas which they conjure up—without thinking about it beforehand, they produce the dharmas straightaway; and these neither come from anywhere, nor do they go anywhere, like magical creations; they think of the past, future, and present as being like things in a dream; dividing their bodies they go to Buddha-fields everywhere, just as the reflection of the sun shining in water is visible everywhere; all their thoughts succeed in being like echoes, which neither come nor go; for them birth-and-death are like parts of a shadow; they realise that what they think is empty; with regard to dharmas they are free of [discriminating] thought; everybody looks up to them; [they regard] everyone as equal and not different; they know all the sutras, and their minds cannot be measured; in all [Buddha-]fields their minds are free of attachment and they have no predilections; they appear in all Buddha-fields without hindrance; they enter the doors of the holding-spells; as for the sutras, they need only hear one to know ten thousand; they are able to accept and keep all the sutras preached by the Buddhas; they wait upon the Buddhas, obtain all the powers of the Buddhas, and obtain all the Buddhas' numinous power; they are brave and fear nothing; their gait is like that of the fierce lion; they are unafraid, speaking 904a
up in all lands; they never forget anything they hear; in debate they are the same as all the Buddhas, not different; they understand all the sutras of original non-being, and are unafraid; if they

wish to obtain the sutras then they immediately know them by themselves, and preach them as indefatigably as the Buddhas; they are the teachers of the world; they are relied upon by all; their conduct is aboveboard, free of insincerity and falseness; they shine brightly in all the [Buddha-]fields; they are not attached to the Three Spheres; their course is unimpeded, among the masses they have no predilections; they have no longing for the dharma of the fundamental limit; by means of all-knowledge they teach others how to enter the Buddha's Way; they are never afraid nor are they frightened; they know all the volumes of the sutras of the Buddha; everyone is blessed in the assemblies which they are in; when they see the very great love of the Buddhas, they rejoice; they are acute in their understanding of the Buddha's sutras which they study; they are fearless in large assemblies; in large assemblies they cannot be surpassed; they are renowned far and wide; they destroy all doubts and difficulties so that everybody understands; they revere the sutras totally; they occupy the lion throne masterfully and teach the Dharma like the Buddhas; they understand all the Buddha's myriad varieties of speech; they immerse themselves in all the myriad million sounds; they love and respect the sutras of the Buddhas; they always think of being by them, and are never separated from the love of the Buddhas; they take pleasure in putting the Buddha's sutras into practice; in coming and going they always follow the Buddha; they always stay at the side of good friends, without ever wearying of them; in the Buddha-fields of the ten quarters there is no place in which they would like to settle; they all undertake the vow and course of action to liberate the myriad people of the ten quarters; their wisdom is a precious thing; they all acquire the body of the treasury of the sutras, which is formless like empty space; they teach others to seek the Way of the bodhisattva, and ensure that the Buddha's line is not cut off; they pursue the Way of the bodhisattva without ever leaving the Mahayana; they attain the Arming with the Great Armor, and the Great Way which is so vast; they quickly attain omniscience, which is praised by all the Buddhas; they approach

the level of the Buddha's ten powers; they penetrate all thoughts; they comprehend all calculations; they understand all the transformations of the world; they understand all success and failure, birth and destruction; they plunge into the sea of sutras with its jewels and, opening up the foremost treasury, they distribute them all; in all [Buddha-]fields they carry out their vows but they do not settle in them; they have very great powers of magical transformation like those which the Buddhas enjoy wielding; within one instant of thought they call to mind the Buddhas all standing before them; in all their goings [to rebirth] they no longer aspire to go, and there is no birthplace [to which they especially aspire]; they see all the incalculable Buddha-fields of the ten quarters; they hear the sutras preached by the Buddhas; they see each and every Buddha with his assembly of monks; yet at this time it is not by means of the vision of the arhats or pratyekabuddhas of the Way of the Immortals that they see, nor is it that they die here
and are born in that Buddha-field and only then see, but right 904b
away while sitting here, they see all the Buddhas and hear all the sutras which the Buddhas preach and they receive them all, just as I now, in the Buddha's presence, see the Buddha face to face, so too the bodhisattvas are never separated from the Buddhas and never fail to hear the sutras?"

The Buddha said to the bodhisattva Bhadrapāla: "Well done! Well done! Many are those who are set free by your question, many are those who are set at rest; they are uncountable among the people of the world. It has brought contentment to them all, above heaven and below it. That you are now able to question the Buddha in this way is because in previous lives, at the time of former Buddhas, you put into practice what you learned and made merit; it is because you made offerings to many Buddhas; it is because you took pleasure in the sutras; it is because you carried out the practice of the Way and kept the precepts; you kept yourself to the practice of the Dharma, pure and uncorrupted; you always fed yourself by begging; you brought many bodhisattvas to realization; you brought bodhisattvas together and instructed them. For this reason you have very great compassion; you have equanimity towards all people; if at any time you wish to see the Buddha, then you see the Buddha; your vows are very great; your conduct is extremely profound; you always keep in mind the wisdom of the Buddha; you keep all the sutras and precepts; you are in full possession of the lineage of the Buddha; your sagely mind is adamantine; you know all the thoughts of the people in the world; you are to be found in the presence of all the Buddhas." The Buddha said to the bodhisattva Bhadrapāla: "Your merits are beyond all reckoning."

The Buddha said: "[There is a meditation called] the Meditation in Which the Buddhas of the Present All Stand Before One. Those who practise this meditation will be able to attain all those things you have asked about."

The bodhisattva Bhadrapāla said to the Buddha: "I pray that the Buddha might, out of his compassion, preach it. If the Buddha were to preach it now, many would be set free, many would be set at rest. I pray that the Buddha might manifest a great light for the sake of bodhisattvas."

The Buddha said to the bodhisattva Bhadrapāla: "There is one Dharma practice which you should always rehearse and preserve, which you should always cultivate without following any other dharmas; which is most exalted and foremost among all meritorious qualities. What is that foremost Dharma practice? It is this meditation called the Meditation in Which the Buddhas of the Present All Stand Before One."

Chapter II

Practice

The Buddha said to the bodhisattva Bhadrapāla: "Any bodhisattvas whose thoughts are at present concentrated and directed towards the Buddhas of the ten quarters, will, if they possess mental concentration, achieve all the exalted practices of a bodhisattva. What is mental concentration? Through compliance with the conditions for reflection on the Buddha, having one's thoughts directed towards the Buddha; having thoughts which are not disturbed, thereby obtaining wisdom; not giving up energy; joining together with good friends in the practice of emptiness; eliminating sleepiness; not congregating; avoiding bad friends; drawing close to good friends; having energy which is not disorderly; in eating, knowing when one has had enough; not craving robes; not begrudging one's own life; being solitary, and avoiding one's relatives; keeping away 904c
from one's home village; practicing equanimity, mastering the attitudes of compassion and rejoicing, and the practice of circumspection; eliminating the coverings; practicing the trances; not following after forms; not taking hold of the dark ones [the five aggregates]; not being absorbed in the diminishers [the twelve sense-fields]; not thinking of the four great ones [the four elements]; not losing one's temper; not being attached to life; eliminating impurity; not forsaking the people of the ten quarters; saving the lives of the people of the ten quarters; regarding the people of the ten quarters as one's own; regarding the people of the ten quarters as not one's own; not wanting to grasp at anything; not altering the precepts; practicing the activity of concentration; wanting to recite the sutras; not falling into violation of the precepts; not

losing one's mental concentration; not doubting the Dharma; not quarreling with the Buddha; not rejecting the Dharma; not causing unrest in the order of monks; avoiding wild talk; assisting men of the Way and of virtue; steering clear of fools; not enjoying or wishing to hear worldly talk; wishing to hear and enjoying all talk of the Way; not wishing to hear that which is produced by taking animals as a basis;[2] practicing the six tastes; performing the five practices; avoiding the ten evils; practicing the ten goods; understanding the nine vexations; practicing the eight forms of energy; discarding the eight forms of sloth; practicing the eight advantages; practicing the nine reflections and the eight thoughts of the man of the Way, yet not becoming attached to trance; not being conceited about one's learning; eliminating pride; listening to the preaching of the Dharma; wishing to hear the sutras; wishing to practise the Dharma; not reckoning things in terms of years; not accepting the conception of a self; avoiding the people of the ten quarters, and not wishing to grasp them; not craving long life; understanding the dark ones [the five aggregates]; not being subject to delusion; not being subject to that which exists; seeking nonaction [nirvana]; not desiring birth-and-death, having great fear of birth-and-death; regarding the dark ones as thieves; regarding the four great ones [the elements] as snakes; regarding the twelve diminishers [the sense-fields] as empty; being in the Triple World for a long time but finding no contentment there; not forgetting the attainment of nonaction; not wanting desires; aspiring to the elimination of birth-and-death; not getting involved in disputes with people; not wishing to fall into birth-and-death; always standing in the presence of Buddhas; regarding the body one receives as a dream; no longer doubting, having acquired faith; doing exactly as one intends; destroying all conceptions; having equanimity towards past, future, and present; always thinking of the meritorious qualities of the Buddhas; submitting to and depending on the Buddha; attaining mastery of mental concentration; not going by the Buddha's bodily marks; regarding all dharmas as one; not arguing with the world; not arguing with one's duty;

gaining understanding of birth according to causes and conditions; succeeding in approving of liberation according to the stage of a Buddha; plunging into the Dharma; by understanding emptiness, thinking of people as neither existing nor perishing; realizing nonaction for oneself; purification of the eye of wisdom; everything being non-dual; having a thought of awakening neither in the middle nor at the sides; all the Buddhas being as one thought; entering a state of freedom from obstruction;[3] having wisdom beyond reproach; through succeeding in understanding the thought of awakening, having a Buddha-wisdom not dependent on others; treating good friends as if they were Buddhas, and not thinking of them as different; being always among bodhisattvas and never 905a
apart from them; being unshakable, even by all Māras; all people being like reflections in a mirror; seeing all the Buddhas as being like pictures; following all the practices of the Dharma; embarking on the pure bodhisattva-course in this way."

The Buddha said: "By virtue of these dharmas of conduct one brings about the meditation and then masters the Meditation in Which the Buddhas of the Present All Stand Before One. By what means does one bring about the Meditation in Which the Buddhas of the Present All Stand Before One? In this way, Bhadrapāla: if there are any monks or nuns, laymen or laywomen who keep the precepts in their entirety, they should settle down somewhere all alone and call to mind the presence of the Buddha Amitābha in the western quarter; then, in accordance with what they have learned, they should reflect that a thousand million myriad Buddha-fields away from here, in his land called Sukhāvatī, in the midst of a host of bodhisattvas, he is preaching the sutras. Let them all constantly call to mind the Buddha Amitābha."

The Buddha said to Bhadrapāla: "It is like a man who goes to sleep and in a dream sees all his gold, silver, and jewels, his parents, brothers, wife and children, relatives and friends, and together with them he amuses himself and enjoys himself immensely. When he wakes up he tells others about it, and afterward he even sheds tears thinking about what he saw in the dream. In the same way, Bhadrapāla, bodhisattvas, whether they be ascetics or wearers of white [laymen or laywomen], having learned of the Buddha-field of Amitābha in the western quarter, should call to mind the Buddha in that quarter. They should not break the precepts, and call him to mind single-mindedly, either for one day and one night, or for seven days and seven nights. After seven days they will see the Buddha Amitābha. If they do not see him in the waking state, then they will see him in a dream.

"It is like the things a man sees in a dream—he is not conscious of day or night, nor is he conscious of inside or outside; he does not fail to see because he is in darkness, nor does he fail to see because there are obstructions. It is the same, Bhadrapāla, for the minds of the bodhisattvas: when they perform this calling to mind, the famous great mountains and the Mount Sumerus in all the Buddha-realms, and all the places of darkness between them, are laid open to them, so that their vision is not obscured, and their minds are not obstructed. These bodhisattvas mahāsattvas do not see through [the obstructions] with the divine eye, nor hear through them with the divine ear, nor travel to that Buddha-field by means of the supernormal power of motion, nor do they die here to be reborn in that Buddha-field there, and only then see; rather, while sitting here they see the Buddha Amitābha, hear the sutras which he preaches, and receive them all. Rising from meditation they are able to preach them to others in full.

"For example, a certain man heard that in the city of Vaiśālī
there was a prostitute called Sumanā; a certain other man heard
about the prostitute Āmrapālī; and a certain other man heard about
905b Utpalavarṇā, who worked as a prostitute. Thereupon they all
longed for them. Those men had never seen these three women, but as soon as they heard about them their lust was aroused. Then, in a dream, they all went to them. On this occasion all three men were in the city of Rājagṛha, thinking about [the women] at the same time, and each of them went in a dream to one of these prostitutes and spent the night together with her. On waking up each one reflected on this."

The Buddha said to Bhadrapāla: "I entrusted the three men to you, who used this incident to preach the sutras to them, so that they understood this wisdom and reached the stage of non-regression from the attainment of the supreme and perfect Way. Afterward they will attain Buddhahood under the name 'Well-Awakened'. In the same way, Bhadrapāla, bodhisattvas hear about the Buddha Amitābha and call him to mind again and again in this land. Because of this calling to mind, they see the Buddha Amitābha. Having seen him they ask him what dharmas it takes to be born in the realm of the Buddha Amitābha. Then the Buddha Amitābha says to these bodhisattvas: 'If you wish to come and be born in my realm, you must always call me to mind again and again, you must always keep this thought in mind without letting up, and thus you will succeed in coming to be born in my realm.'" The Buddha said: "Because of this calling to mind of the Buddha, these bodhisattvas will succeed in being born in the realm of the Buddha Amitābha. They should always call him to mind in this way: 'The Buddha's body is endowed with all the thirty-two marks, he radiates light, he is fine and upstanding beyond compare, in the midst of the assembly of monks he preaches the sutras, and the sutras he preaches are of indestructible form.[4] What is of indestructible form? Feelings, thoughts, birth-and-death, consciousness, spirits, earth, water, fire and wind, the world and the heavens above, up as far as Brahmā and Mahābrahmā, are of indestructible form.' Because of calling the Buddha to mind, one obtains the meditation of emptiness. Such is the calling to mind of the Buddha."

The Buddha said to the bodhisattva Bhadrapāla: "Who is to bear witness to the meditation? My disciple Mahākāśyapa, the bodhisattva Indradatta, the devaputra Susīma, together with those who at this time know this meditation—any who have practised and mastered this meditation bear witness to it. What is it to which they bear witness? They bear witness to this meditation knowing it to be the concentration of emptiness."

The Buddha said to Bhadrapāla: "Once in time past there was a Buddha by the name of Xubori. At that time a certain man went

on a journey, which took him into a vast marshy wilderness where he was unable to get anything to eat or drink. Hungry and thirsty, he fell asleep, and then in a dream he obtained luscious delicacies. After eating and drinking he awoke, and his belly was empty. 'Is not everything that exists like a dream?' he reflected to himself." The Buddha said: "Through reflecting on emptiness, that man then and there attained happiness in dharmas which do not come into existence from anywhere, and straightaway attained non-regression. In the same way, Bhadrapāla, bodhisattvas hear of the Buddha of the present in whatever quarter they are facing, and constantly
905c reflect on that quarter, wishing to see the Buddha. When they reflect on the Buddha they ought not to reflect on [him as] an existing thing, nor should they have [the notion: 'It is something'] set up by me. As they would conceive of emptiness so should they reflect on the Buddha standing there, like a precious gem set on beryl. In this way bodhisattvas will have a clear vision of the innumerable Buddhas of the ten quarters.

"It is like a man who travels afar to another land, and thinks about his native place, his family, his relatives, and his property. In a dream that man returns to his native place, sees his family and relatives, and enjoys talking to them. After seeing them in the dream he wakes up and tells his friends about it: 'I went back to my native place and saw my family and relatives.'" The Buddha said: "So it is with the bodhisattvas. If they hear the name of the Buddha in whatever quarter they are facing, and constantly reflect on that quarter, wishing to see the Buddha, then the bodhisattvas see all the Buddhas, like a precious gem placed on beryl.

"It is like a monk contemplating the bones of the dead laid out before him. At times he contemplates them when they are green. At times he contemplates them when they are white. At times he contemplates them when they are red. At times he contemplates them when they are black. Nobody brings these bones to him, nor do these bones exist, nor do they come from anywhere. They exist only as thoughts produced by the mind. So it is with the bodhisattvas who possess the numinous power of the Buddha and are established in the meditation: whatever the quarter in which they wish to see a Buddha, if they wish to see him they do so. Why? It is thus, Bhadrapāla: this meditation has been perfected by the Buddha's power. Those who possess the numinous power of the Buddha and who are established in the meditation have three things: they possess the numinous power of the Buddha, they possess the power of the Buddha's meditation, and they possess the power of their former merit. Because of these three things they succeed in seeing the Buddha.

"Bhadrapāla, it is like a young man, upright and handsome, who adorns himself. Wishing to see his own reflection, he either takes a clean vessel and fills it with fine hempseed oil, or takes a fine vessel and fills it with clear water, or a newly polished mirror, or a flawless crystal. Thereupon he reflects himself and sees his own reflection. What would you say, Bhadrapāla? When the man is reflected in the hempseed oil, the water, the mirror or the crystal, could it possibly be that the reflection enters them from outside?"

Bhadrapāla said: "No, God among Gods. It is simply because the hempseed oil, the crystal, the water, or the mirror are clean and pure that he sees his own reflection. His reflection neither emerges from within nor enters from outside."

The Buddha said: "Well done! Well done, Bhadrapāla! So it is, Bhadrapāla. When the forms are clear, everything is clear. If one wishes to see the Buddha then one sees him. If one sees him then one asks questions. If one asks then one is answered, one hears the sutras and rejoices greatly. One reflects thus: 'Where did the Buddha come from? Where did I go to?' and one thinks to oneself: 'The Buddha came from nowhere, and I also went nowhere.' One thinks to oneself: 'The Three Realms—the Realm of Desire, the Realm of Form, and the Realm of the Formless—these Three Realms are simply made by thought. Whatever I think, that I see. 906a
The mind creates the Buddha. The mind itself sees him. The mind is the Buddha. The mind is the Tathāgata. The mind is my body, the mind sees the Buddha. The mind does not itself know the mind, the mind does not itself see mind. A mind with conceptions is stupidity,

a mind without conceptions is nirvana. There is nothing in these dharmas which can be enjoyed; they are all made by thinking. If thinking is nothing but empty, then anything which is thought is also utterly nonexistent.' So it is, Bhadrapāla, such is the vision of the bodhisattvas who are established in the meditation."

The Buddha then recited the following verses:

> Mind does not know mind;
> With mind one cannot see mind.
> Mind giving rise to conceptions is stupidity;
> Free of conceptions it is nirvana.
>
> There is nothing fixed or firm in these dharmas;
> They are forever located in thinking.
> When one understands emptiness,
> One is altogether free of conceptual thinking.

Chapter III

The Four Things

"If bodhisattvas possess four things or dharmas, they quickly master this meditation. What are the four? First, no one can destroy their faith. Second, no one can withstand their energy. Third, no one can match the wisdom they attain. Fourth, they always devote themselves to good teachers. These are the four.

"If bodhisattvas possess a further four things, they quickly master this meditation. What are the four? First, for three months they ought not to have a worldly thought, even for the time it takes to snap the fingers. Second, for three months they ought not to go to sleep, even for the time it takes to snap the fingers. Third, continually walking, they should not stop or sit down for three months, except for around mealtimes. Fourth, in preaching the sutras to others, they should not expect clothes or food and drink from them. These are the four.

"If bodhisattvas possess a further four things, they quickly master this meditation. What are the four? First, they gather people together and come to the Buddha. Second, they gather people together and cause them to hear the sutras. Third, they are not envious. Fourth, they teach people to study the Way of the Buddha. These are the four.

"If bodhisattvas possess a further four things, they quickly master this meditation. What are the four? First, they make an image of the Buddha or they make a picture, for the sake of this meditation. Second, for the sake of this meditation, they take a fine length of plain silk and have somebody copy this meditation. Third, they teach conceited people to enter the Buddha's Way.

Fourth, they always preserve the Buddha's Dharma. These are the four."

Then the Buddha recited the following verses of commendation: "You should always rejoice in and believe in the Buddha's Dharma. Recite the sutras and reflect on emptiness, without settling down therein.
906b tling down therein. Be energetic and eliminate sleepiness. For three months you should not sit down out of laziness. When the sutras are preached accept them and study them calmly and carefully. You should do your utmost to spread them far and wide. If anyone gives you presents or offers you food, you should not be pleased. If you do not covet anything, you will quickly obtain the sutra. The Buddha's complexion is as radiant as gold. His body has thirty-two marks, and each mark has one hundred blessings or merits. He is fine and upstanding, as if made out of heavenly gold. Commit yourself in advance to all the Buddhas of the past and the Buddhas of the future. Always think of and make offerings to the Buddhas of the present, who are all the most exalted of men. You should make offerings to the Buddha complete with flowers, perfumes, powdered incense, and food. You should have good thoughts. Because of this, the meditation will not be far away. With the constant music of drums and the music of singing girls,[5] you should always rejoice in the Buddha-mind, since you seek this meditation. You should make images of the Buddha, perfect in various ways and beautiful in various ways, with countenances as radiant as gold. If you seek this meditation, you should always take pleasure in giving. In keeping the precepts you should be pure, and lofty in conduct. Eliminate sloth, and before long you will quickly master this meditation. Do not give rise to anger, always act lovingly, always act compassionately, be equal-minded, and have no hatred, and presently, before long, you will master this meditation. Love your good teachers utterly, regarding them as Buddhas. You ought to be free of anger and covetousness. You should not be grasping with the gift of the sutras. So is it taught. You should hold firmly to all the sutra-dharmas, and you should immerse yourself in all of them according to this. This is the Way and the path

of all the Buddhas. They who proceed in this manner shall presently, before long, master the meditation."

The Buddha said to Bhadrapāla: "In this way bodhisattvas should be loving and cheerful towards good teachers, should regard their teachers as Buddhas, and should provide them with every service. When they wish to write out this meditation sutra, or when they wish to study it, bodhisattvas should honor their teachers in this way. Bhadrapāla, if bodhisattvas should get angry at their good teachers, if they should find fault with their good teachers, or not regard their good teachers as Buddhas, they will have difficulty in mastering the meditation.

"Bhadrapāla, it is like a clear-sighted man who gazes at the constellations at midnight and sees the stars in great profusion. In the same way, Bhadrapāla, when the bodhisattvas who possess the numinous power of the Buddha and are established in the meditation look towards the east, they see many hundreds of Buddhas, many thousands of Buddhas, many myriads of Buddhas, many millions of Buddhas; and in the same way they see all the Buddhas of the ten quarters as well."

The Buddha said to Bhadrapāla: "These bodhisattvas, like the eyes of the Buddha, know all and see all. Thus, Bhadrapāla, these bodhisattvas who wish to master the Meditation in Which the Buddhas of the Present All Stand Before One will become perfectly endowed with liberality, the same with keeping the precepts, their persons will become perfectly endowed with forbearance, energy, single-mindedness, wisdom, and the wisdom of liberation." 906c

Then the Buddha spoke the following words of commendation: "Just as a clear-sighted man looks up at midnight at the innumerable constellations, and, thinking about them by day, sees them all, so too the bodhisattvas who master the meditation see innumerable hundreds and thousands of Buddhas, and, having awoken from the meditation, call them all to mind and see them; at will they speak of them to the disciples." The Buddha said: "Just as my vision is clear and always sees the world, so too the bodhisattvas, once they have mastered the meditation, see innumerable Buddhas.

When they see the Buddhas they do not look at their bodily marks, they only look at their ten powers. Unlike worldly people who have cravings, they have destroyed all the poisons, are pure, and no longer think [conceptually]. Such are the meritorious qualities which the bodhisattvas attain. They listen to this sutra and comply with this sutra as if it were nirvana. Hearing that these dharmas are utterly empty, they are without fear. I shall provide this preaching of the sutra for the sake of the mass of people, causing them all to attain the Way of the Buddha." The Buddha said: "Just as my monk Ānanda is wise and retains sutras as soon as he hears them, so too the bodhisattvas who master this meditation, hearing innumerable volumes of sutras, retain them all." The Bud-
907a dha said: "Just as the bodhisattvas in the Buddha-field of Amitābha always see innumerable Buddhas, so too the bodhisattvas who master the meditation always see innumerable Buddhas. Always be compassionate in your faith. Just as a thirsty man longs for a drink, always have exceedingly great love. Discard common worldly things, and always take pleasure in the gift of the sutras. Therefore you will be pure and will master the meditation before long."

Chapter IV

Similes

The Buddha said to Bhadrapāla: "If the bodhisattvas who lovingly seek the meditation do not practise this meditation energetically once they have obtained it, it is, Bhadrapāla, like a man who loads up a ship with precious gems with the intention of transporting them over the ocean; before arriving, the ship is wrecked midway; and the men of Jambudvīpa are all stricken with grief, thinking: 'So many precious gems of ours are lost!'—in the same way, Bhadrapāla, once these bodhisattvas hear this meditation, if they do not copy it, study it, recite it, or keep it in conformity with the Dharma, then all the gods and the people will be stricken with grief and will lament: 'So many precious sutras of ours are thus lost, because of the loss of this profound meditation!'" The Buddha said: "This meditation sutra is ordained by the Buddha and it is commended by the Buddha. Those who hear this profound meditation sutra, and do not copy it, study it, recite it, cultivate it, or keep it in conformity with the Dharma, are perverse and stupid. They have a high opinion of themselves and will not accept this sutra. They have their minds set on high ability, yet they are not willing to study this meditation.

"Bhadrapāla, it is like a stupid boy who is given a handful of sandalwood incense by someone. Unwilling to accept it, he perversely tells him that it is dirty. The seller of sandalwood incense says to that person: 'Sir, you aren't saying that this sandalwood incense is dirty, are you? If you were to take it and smell it, you would know whether or not it was fragrant, and if you were to look at it you would know whether or not it was pure.' The fool shuts his eyes so as not to look, and he refuses to smell it." The

Buddha said: "Those who hear this meditation, who are similarly unwilling to accept it, and who perversely reject it, they are people who do not keep the precepts. Those who reject this precious jewel of a sutra are stupid and unwise, they regard their own attainment of perfection in the trances as transcendence, they perversely claim that the world exists, they do not immerse themselves in emptiness or know nonbeing. When these people hear this meditation they do not rejoice in it, have faith in it, or immerse themselves in it. On the contrary, they make contemptuous remarks: 'Can the Buddha have such profound sutras? And can he have such numinous power?' On the contrary, they deride it: 'Could there be in the world any monks of the likes of Ānanda?'" The Buddha said: "These people go away from those who possess this meditation, and in twos and threes say to each other: 'What kind of preachings
907b are these discourses? Where did they get these discourses from? It is simply that they got together and made up these discourses themselves, that's all. This sutra was not preached by the Buddha.'"

The Buddha said to Bhadrapāla: "It is like a merchant who shows a stupid peasant boy a pearl, and he asks the merchant: 'How much money is this worth?' The merchant replies: 'Place this pearl in the darkness in a dark place at midnight and just fill the area lit up by its radiance with jewels.'" The Buddha said: "That person doesn't understand its value at all; instead he derides this pearl, saying 'Could its value be the same as one ox? Could you possibly exchange an ox for it? I think it can't be more than this. If you'll give it to me, well and good. If you don't want to, there's an end to it.' Thus, Bhadrapāla, those who hear this meditation and do not have faith in it perversely deride this sutra in the same way."

The Buddha said: "If the bodhisattvas who possess this meditation, accept it, and believe in it then put it into practice, they will be protected on all four sides, will have nothing to fear, will be perfect in keeping the precepts, will obtain great brilliance, will have deeply penetrating wisdom, and will preach it to other people. Bodhisattvas should share and discuss this meditation with others, and pass it on from one person to the next. They should ensure that this meditation endures for a long time."

The Buddha said: "The stupid people, even though they have not made offerings under the Buddhas of former generations and have not made merit, are nevertheless conceited, and engage in much slander and jealousy, for the sake of material gain. They only wish to court fame, they only wish to make a noise. They do not acquire a good teacher, nor do they understand the sutras. When they hear this meditation they do not have faith in it, rejoice in it, or immerse themselves in it. On the contrary, they slander it to others, saying 'It is just that those shameless people have made this sutra for themselves. This sutra was not preached by the Buddha.'"

The Buddha said to Bhadrapāla: "I now tell you this, Bhadrapāla. If a seeker of the Way of the bodhisattva, either a good young man or a good woman, were to fill these three thousand lands with precious gems and offer them to the Buddha, any such merit would not be as good as hearing this meditation. If any bodhisattvas were to hear this meditation, believe in it, and rejoice in it, then the increase in their blessings would be so much greater."

Then the Buddha spoke the following words of commendation: "If these three thousand lands were filled with precious gems and offered to the Buddha, so as to seek Buddhahood thereby; and if there were another man who took up this meditation, which the Buddha has praised, who heard it and believed in it, the increase in his blessings would be greater." The Buddha said: "These deluded and conceited men, unbelievers and followers of bad friends, do not believe in or rejoice in this sutra when they hear it. They are no different from the enemies of my sutras. These men who do not keep the precepts are sunk in arrogance. One after the other,
other men hear their words, believe, and follow them. This is to 907c
destroy the Buddha's Dharma. Those men say to each other: 'This sutra was not preached by the Buddha.' They utter this slander outright." The Buddha said: "If anyone believes in this meditation, that person has seen past Buddhas in former lives. It is just for the sake of these believers that I therefore preach this meditation. Such people as those always preserve the Buddha's Dharma. Those who hear this sutra, believe in it, and rejoice in it, you should know that they are not far from Buddhahood. Those who keep the

precepts strictly are always true-hearted and honor the sutras. It is just for the sake of these people that I therefore preach."

The Buddha said to Bhadrapāla: "It is exactly as I say. It is for this reason only that I preach this discourse. As for those who now see me preaching this meditation, if in future lives they hear this meditation they will never doubt it, will not laugh at it derisively, will not say they do not believe it, unless they are with bad teachers. Even if they are with good teachers, such people as those whose merit is meager will increasingly devote themselves to bad teachers, and when they hear this meditation, these people will not believe in it or rejoice in it or immerse themselves in it. Why? They do not believe, simply because they have not studied for long, they have not experienced many Buddhas, and they have little faith or wisdom."

The Buddha said to Bhadrapāla: "If there are bodhisattvas who, hearing this meditation, do not laugh at it derisively and do not slander it, but rejoice in it, do not fall into doubt, do not say that they believe it one moment and disbelieve it the next, but take pleasure in copying it, take pleasure in studying it, take pleasure in reciting it, take pleasure in keeping it," the Buddha said, "I have foreknown and foreseen them all. These people have not made merit under just one Buddha, nor under two or three or ten—they have all heard this meditation under a hundred Buddhas. If, when they hear this meditation at a future time, they copy, study, recite and keep the volumes of the sutra, and finally cultivate it for one day and one night, their blessings will be incalculable, they will attain non-regression, and they will fulfill their aspirations."

The Buddha said to Bhadrapāla: "Listen as I teach a simile. Bhadrapāla, it is like a man who takes one Buddha-field and pounds it all to atoms of dust. Taking one atom of this dust, he again pounds it all into as many atoms as there are atoms of dust in one Buddha-field. Taking all of those atoms of dust, each and every one of them, he again pounds them all into as many atoms as there are atoms of dust in one Buddha-field. What would you say,
908a Bhadrapāla—would there be a great number of these atoms of

dust?" Bhadrapāla said: "A very great number, a very great number, God among Gods." The Buddha said to Bhadrapāla: "I cite this simile for you all. If a bodhisattva takes each of these atoms of dust and puts it in a Buddha-field, fills with precious gems that number of Buddha-fields, and uses them all as an offering to the Buddhas, it is not as good as hearing this meditation. If another bodhisattva, when he hears this meditation, copies it, studies it, recites it, keeps it, or preaches it to other people, even for a moment, that bodhisattva's merit is incalculable." The Buddha said: "Those who possess this meditation, who copy, study, recite, and keep it, and preach it to other people—if the blessings for them are such, how much more would they be for those who cultivate this meditation and perfect it?"

The Buddha then recited the following verses:

Although one fills with jewels and makes a donation
Of the Three Thousand Great Thousand Realms,
If one does not hear such a sutra as this,
One's merit and blessings will be paltry.

Any bodhisattvas who seek much merit
Should teach and take up the practice of this meditation;
If they are quick to believe and recite this sutra-dharma,
Their merit and blessings will be infinite.

If worlds as numerous as the atoms of dust in one
  Buddha-land
Were all pounded to pieces and reduced to atoms of dust,
And Buddha-lands exceeding their number
Were filled with precious gems and used as a gift;

And if someone were to take up and preach to others
The meaning of four lines from the Lord of the World
  herein,
This meditation being the wisdom of all the Buddhas,
The merit of getting to hear it would be beyond
  comparison;

Not to mention those who expounded it themselves,
Took it up, recited it, reflected on it even for a moment,
Or made ever-increasing progress in their practice of it:
Their merit and blessings would be beyond measure.

Even if everybody were to become Buddhas,
Pure in sagely knowledge, foremost in wisdom,
And all for millions of aeons, and more,
Were to expound the merit of one verse,

And were to extol its blessings until their nirvana,
Singing its praises for countless millions of aeons,
They would not be able to exhaust the merit
Connected with one verse from this meditation.

If the area of all Buddha-lands
In the four quarters, the four intermediate points,
the zenith and the nadir,
Were filled with precious gems and used as a gift,
So as to make an offering to the Buddha, the God
among Gods,

And if someone were to hear this meditation,
The blessings he would obtain would exceed that;
As for those who recited and expounded it calmly and
carefully,
Their merit could not be conveyed by any analogy.

Conceit never arises in them,
Nor do they ever pursue an evil destiny;
They understand the profound Dharma, and are not
enmeshed in doubt;
Such are the results of practicing this meditation.

908b The scholars thereby see and honor me;
With their great virtue and energy, they are attached to
nothing;
They increase their faith and understanding as
bodhisattvas;

They strive to study the meditation extolled by the
Buddha.

I charge you, I exhort you always:
Strive to act energetically, without being idle,
Rouse yourselves bravely, practise with diligence,
So that attaining the Great Way will not be far off.

Those who recite and accept this meditation
Have already seen a hundred thousand Buddhas face
to face.
If during the great terror, at the very end,
They possess this meditation, they will have no fear.

The monk who practises this thereby sees me.
He always follows the Buddha and is not separated
from him.
The bodhisattva who hears and practises the meditation
Is duty-bound to preserve it and preach it to others.

If bodhisattvas obtain this meditation,
Then and only then are they called 'ones of all-embracing
wisdom';
Since they have attained the holding-spell praised by the
Buddha,
They shall quickly perfect the Way of the Buddha and
wisdom like the sea.

Constantly recite and preach this meditation;
Follow the Buddha's Dharma, the teaching of the Lord
of the World:
Hearing its lineage one attains full awakening,
Exactly in accordance with what the Buddha has
preached.

Here Ends Fascicle One
of The Pratyutpanna Samādhi Sutra

Fascicle Two

Chapter V

Nonattachment

The Buddha said to Bhadrapāla: "How should this meditation for bodhisattvas be undertaken? Just as I, the Buddha, am now preaching sutras in your presence, bodhisattvas should think that the Buddhas are all standing before them; they should call to mind in full the Buddhas, who are upright, whom everyone wants to see. They should think of each and every mark, recalling that no one can see the tops of the Buddhas' heads. They should think of all this in full, and they will see the Buddhas. They should think: 'I myself will also be like this, I will also acquire such bodily marks as these, and will also attain such morality and meditation as these.' They should think: 'Will I attain this through the mind or will I attain it through my body?' They should think again: 'The Buddha did not attain it by means of the mind, nor did he attain it by means of the body. Buddhahood is not attained by means of the mind, nor is it attained by means of form. Why? As for mind, the Buddha has no mind; as for form, the Buddha has no form. It is not by means of this mind and form that one attains supreme and 908c
perfect awakening. Why? The Buddha's form has come to an end, the Buddha's feelings, conceptions, birth-and-death, and consciousness have come to an end, and what the Buddha preaches has

come to an end, which is not perceived or known by fools, but is understood by the wise.' They should think: 'What kind of thoughts should one have to attain Buddhahood? Should one attain Buddhahood by means of the body, or should one attain it by means of wisdom?' Furthermore, they should think: 'One does not attain Buddhahood through the body, nor does one attain it through wisdom.' Why? If one looks for wisdom one cannot find it. Even if one looks for the 'I', it cannot ever be found. Nothing is attained, nothing is seen. All dharmas are originally nonexistent. To think that they exist causes attachment. If they do not exist, to say perversely that they do is also attachment. One neither thinks of these two, nor does one incline to what is between them. It is for this reason alone that they are not on either side, nor in the middle, they neither exist, nor do they not exist. Why? All dharmas are empty; they are like nirvana; they are indestructible, imperishable, and unsteady; they are neither here nor there; they are markless; they are unwavering. What does it mean to say they are unwavering? Wise men cannot calculate them, therefore they are unwavering. Thus, Bhadrapāla, when the bodhisattvas see the Buddha, the thoughts in the bodhisattvas' minds are free of attachment. Why? I have preached nonexistence, the sutras preach nonexistence, and if one is not attached to that, has destroyed the root and cut off the root, this is nonattachment. Thus, Bhadrapāla, these bodhisattvas who cultivate this meditation should have this vision of the Buddha, yet they should not become attached to the Buddha. Why? If they have any attachments they will burn themselves. It is like a great lump of iron placed in a fire and heated until it is red: no wise person would grasp it with his hand. Why? It would burn a person's hand. In the same way, Bhadrapāla, if they see the Buddha the bodhisattvas will not become attached to him; and they will not become attached to form, feelings, conceptions, birth-and-death, and consciousness. Why? Those who become attached burn themselves. If they see the Buddha they should simply reflect on his merits, and they should seek the Mahayana." The Buddha said to Bhadrapāla: "These bodhisattvas should not have any attachments in the meditation. If they do not become attached they will quickly master this meditation."

The Buddha then recited the following verses:

As in a newly polished mirror, or in a vessel filled with oil,
A woman, adorning herself, reflects her own form
And, conceiving lustful thoughts for it,
Abandons all restraint, becoming utterly infatuated;

She pursues what is not real, rejecting the Dharma
for nothing;
On account of form she runs about, setting her body
on fire;
The woman's troubles arise from this,
Because she does not understand that dharmas are
impermanent and empty.

So too the bodhisattva with conceptual thoughts: 909a
"I shall attain Buddhahood and get its sweet dew,
And liberate people from misery and trouble."
Because he has the concept of "person" he lacks
understanding.

If one searches for the basis of a person, it cannot be
apprehended,
And it does not undergo birth-and-death or nirvana;
Dharmas are ungraspable, like the moon in water;
If one contemplates the Way of the Buddha, there is
nothing that one can depend on.

Wise bodhisattvas ought to understand this,
And realise that the whole world is nonexistent from
the beginning.
Free of attachments to all human creations,
They quickly attain the Way of the Buddha in this world.

All Buddhas realized the Way through mind.
The mind is pure, bright, and unsullied;

Pristine in the five destinies, it does not suffer the
limitations of form;
Anyone who understands this perfects the Great Way.

All dharmas are free of form and of the corrupting
influences;
Divorced from conceptual thought, they are empty; free of
conceptual thought, they are empty.
If one cuts off lust, one then liberates the mind.
Anyone who understands this masters the meditation.

Energetically practise, aspiring to the Buddha's body;
Always listen to the dharmas which are fundamentally
pure;
Do not practise aspiringly, and do not lack aspiration,[6]
And this meditation will not be hard to master.

Contemplate all that exists as being like empty space;
The thought of the Way is tranquil and preeminently
fine;
It is free of conceptual thought, free of construction, and
free of hearing;
This is to comprehend the noble Way of the Buddha.

Seeing all forms one is free of conceptual thought,
One's vision is free of attachment, and does not come and
go;
If one always contemplates the Buddhas as equal to
emptiness,
One has already transcended the aspirations of the world.

Those people who are pure, whose vision is unsullied,
Who practise energetically, and are always tranquil,
Receive incalculable sutra-dharmas,
And reflect on this meditation with clear discernment.

Practicing this meditation they are free of attachment;
They dispel all darkness and achieve mental concentration;

They do not see the Heroes of the World; for them there
are no worthies and sages;
The followers of heterodox ways are confused when they
hear this.

Transcending conceptual thought they should strive
resolutely;
With a pure mind they will succeed in seeing the Buddhas;
Once they have seen the Buddhas they will not see them
again;
Only then will they understand this noble meditation.

Earth, water, fire—nothing can obstruct them;
Wind and empty space cannot block them either;
They who practise this energetically will see the ten
quarters;
Sitting down, they will hear at a distance and receive the
Dharmas that are taught.

Just as I expound the sutras here,
And those who delight in the Dharma of the Way see the
Buddha face to face,
They who undertake the practice zealously and are free of
attachment
Follow only the Dharma preached by the Lord of the World.

In this way the practitioners are free of thought,
Listen only to the message of the Way and undertake the
gift of the Dharma,
Always reflect on and understand this meditation,
And everywhere carefully receive and recite what the
Buddha has expounded.

All past Buddhas have discussed the Dharma,
As will future Lords of the World:
They expound, disseminate, and analyze the meaning; 909b
Together they all extol this meditation.

I too like this am Lord among Men,
Supreme in the world, the father of beings;
I know and understand all—this is the vision of the Way;
Therefore I explain and reveal the tranquil meditation.

Anyone who recites and accepts this meditation
Will always enjoy physical ease and mental composure;
These are the incalculable virtues of the Buddha;
They ensure that it will not be hard to acquire the noble Way of the Buddha.

Widely they gather an inconceivable host of sutras,
Wishing to penetrate the teachings of all the Buddhas;
Quickly they eliminate desire and all impurities
And energetically practise this pure meditation.

In the present world they wish to see innumerable Buddhas,
They take pleasure in hearing and receiving the Dharma from the Lords.
Quickly they eliminate form and get rid of attachments,
And practise this pure and tranquil meditation.

Here they have no lust or anger,
They avoid stupidity and renounce hatred and love,
They get rid of unwisdom and eliminate suspicion,
Thus they acquire an understanding of the tranquil meditation.

Chapter VI

The Four Classes

The bodhisattva Bhadrapāla said to the Buddha: "How marvellous is the preaching of the meditation by the God among Gods! If any bodhisattva who has renounced desire to become a monk should hear this meditation, how should he study it, how should he keep it, and how should he practise it?"

The Buddha said: "If any bodhisattva who has renounced desire to become a monk wants to study this meditation, recite this meditation, and keep this meditation, he should be pure in keeping the precepts, and he ought not to deviate from the precepts by so much as a hair's breadth. What is meant by a bodhisattva's not deviating from the precepts? He keeps all the prohibitory rules; he should keep all the rules for going out, coming in, and walking; he ought not to transgress the precepts by so much as a hair's breadth, and he should always fear and avoid insincerity; he should keep all the prohibitions. To keep them like this is to be pure in the keeping of the precepts. What is meant by a bodhisattva's deviating from the precepts? Such a bodhisattva looks for form. What is looking for form? This person thinks: 'By means of this merit may I in a future rebirth become either a god or a universal monarch.'" The Buddha said: "Because of this the bodhisattva-monk deviates from the precepts. He always uses this practice, uses these precepts, and uses the blessings derived from self-control to aspire to a place of rebirth and to enjoy his desires. This is deviating from the precepts."

The Buddha said to Bhadrapāla: "The bodhisattva-monk who wishes to study this meditation should be pure in keeping the precepts, he should be perfect in keeping the precepts, he should not

be insincere in keeping the precepts, he should be praised by the wise, he should be praised by the arhats, he should give the gift of the sutras, he should be energetic, his mindfulness should be strong,
909c he should be full of faith and inspiration; he should serve his preceptors, he should serve his good teachers. The person from whom he hears this meditation, in whatever place he is able to hear this meditation, he should regard him as a Buddha." The Buddha said to Bhadrapāla: "If this bodhisattva regards his teacher as he would regard the Buddha, he will master the meditation quickly. If he does not honor his good teacher, if he is disrespectful to his good teacher and imposes upon him, then even if he studies this meditation for a long time, keeps it for a long time, and practises it for a long time, if he does not honor his good teacher he will quickly lose it." The Buddha said to Bhadrapāla: "This bodhisattva should regard as a Buddha whatever monk, nun, layman, or laywoman he gets to hear this meditation from, and he should venerate the place where he hears the meditation."

The Buddha said to Bhadrapāla: "Wherever the bodhisattva hears this meditation he should not have any insincere intentions; this bodhisattva should not have any insincere thoughts, he should always take pleasure in staying by himself, not begrudge his own life, he should not hanker after the things that others desire, he should always practise begging for his food, not accept invitations, not be jealous, maintain self-control, abide in accordance with the Dharma, incline to contentment with what he has and nothing more, should keep walking without letting up, and should not go to sleep—in this way, Bhadrapāla, in accordance with the teachings in this sutra, he who renounces desire to become a monk and studies this meditation should act like this and cultivate it like this."

The bodhisattva Bhadrapāla said to the Buddha: "How marvellous is the Dharma preached by the God among Gods! At a later time there will be some lazy bodhisattvas who, when they hear this meditation, will not want to exert themselves. They will think to themselves. 'We shall look for this meditation at a later time, under future Buddhas. Why? Because our bodies are thin and infirm in the extreme. We fear that we are unable to strive for it.' When they hear this sutra they will be lazy and will not exert themselves. There will also be some energetic bodhisattvas who will wish to study this sutra, will teach it, and will teach it in accordance with the Dharma of this sutra. Because of this sutra they will not begrudge their persons or their lives, and they will not hanker after the possessions of others. If people praise them they will not for that reason be pleased. They will not be addicted to bowls or robes, they will have no longings, they will always be free of desires. Hearing this sutra they will not be lazy, but always exert themselves. Those people will not think: 'We shall only strive for it later, under future Buddhas.' They will think to themselves: 'Even if it makes our sinews, marrow and flesh all shrivel up, we will study this meditation without ever slackening!' They will think to themselves. 'We shall never die lazy!' When they hear this sutra they will all rejoice."

Then the Buddha said: "Well done! Well done, Bhadrapāla! It is exactly as you have said. I shall help them to rejoice, and all the Buddhas of the past, future, and present will help them to rejoice." 910a

The Buddha then recited the following verses:

If one fully accepts and studies the Dharma
I am now preaching, and abides in solitude,
Pursuing meritorious conduct and exercising
  self-restraint,
This meditation will not be hard to master.

Always beg for food, do not accept invitations;
Renounce all desires and pleasures;
Honor as you would the Lord of the World, the
  Dharma teacher
From whom you hear this meditation.

They who recite and practise this meditation
Are always energetic, not lazy.
They must not be grudging with the sutra-dharma:
Without angling for offerings, they give the sutra.

If one accepts this meditation,
One is then a son of this Buddha.
They who study and practise it in this way
Never take long to master the meditation.

Be ever zealous, not lazy;
Eliminate sleep, set free the mind.
You should avoid bad friends,
Then practise according to this Dharma.

Discard self-indulgence, do not rest,
Always avoid the congregating of the multitude.
Monks who strive for this meditation
Should do this, in accordance with the Buddha's teaching.

The bodhisattva Bhadrapāla said to the Buddha. "As for the nun seeking the Way of the bodhisattva, who wishes to study this meditation and cultivate it—what dharmas should she establish herself in to study and cultivate this meditation?"

The Buddha said to Bhadrapāla: "The nun who seeks to set out in the Mahayana, and who studies and cultivates this meditation, should be modest and respectful, should not be envious, should not get angry, should eliminate conceit, eliminate haughtiness, refrain from laziness, should be energetic, get rid of sleepiness, should not go to sleep, renounce all possessions, should keep herself ever pure, should not be sparing of her person or her life, should always rejoice in the sutras, should strive for great learning, should get rid of lust, anger, and stupidity, get out of Māra's net, should get rid of her beloved clothes, ornaments, beads, and rings, should not be foul-mouthed, should not covet fine bowls or robes, should be praised by others, and should not be insincere. When she studies this meditation, she should honor her good teachers and regard them as Buddhas; she should accept the teachings of this sutra and cultivate this meditation."

The Buddha then recited the following verses:

If a nun conducts herself respectfully,
Is not envious and avoids anger,

Eliminates arrogance and gets rid of haughtiness—
If she conducts herself in this way she masters the
meditation.

She should be energetic and eliminate sleepiness,
Renounce desire and not covet long life,
Be single-minded in loving this Dharma— 910b
If she seeks the meditation, so should she act.

She must not give in to lustful thoughts,
She must do away with anger and stupidity,
She must not fall into Māra's net—
If she seeks the meditation, so should she act.

If anyone studies this meditation,
She should not be flirtatious, and reject carnal desire;
She should renounce all suspicions;
She should be sincere and not meretricious.

Rejecting inferior love, she has always the greater love;
She honors the good teacher selflessly;
She should avoid all evils—
If she seeks the meditation, so should she act.

If she strives for the Dharma and wishes to master it,
She should not be attached to bowls and robes,
And should regard as no different from the Buddha
The person from whom she hears this meditation.

The bodhisattva Bhadrapāla said to the Buddha: "If a bodhisattva wearing white, one who cultivates the Way living in the home, should wish, when he hears this meditation, to study it and cultivate it, how should he establish himself in the Dharma so as to study and cultivate this meditation?"

The Buddha said to Bhadrapāla: "The bodhisattva wearing white, who, on hearing this meditation, wishes to study and cultivate it, should hold firmly to the five precepts and remain pure; he should not drink wine, nor give it to other people to drink; he should not have intercourse with women—he should not do it himself, nor should he advise other people to do it; he should not have any affection for his wife and children; he should not long for sons and daughters; he should not long for property; he should always think longingly of abandoning his wife and children and undertaking the life of an ascetic; he should always maintain the eightfold fast, and at the time of the fast he should always keep the fast at a Buddhist monastery; he should always think of giving, and not think: 'I myself shall obtain blessings from it', but give for the sake of the myriad people; he should always have great love for his good teacher; if he sees a monk who keeps the precepts he should not be disrespectful to him or speak ill of him. When he has conducted himself in this way, he should study and cultivate this meditation."

The Buddha then recited the following verses:

If a bodhisattva living in the home
Wishes to master this meditation,
He should always study it thoroughly,
Without any cravings in his heart.

When he recites this meditation,
He should think eagerly of becoming an ascetic;
He should not desire his wife and children,
And he should renounce property and sex.

He should always uphold the five precepts
And the eightfold fast for one whole day;
At the time of the fast, in a Buddhist monastery,
He should study the meditation with acute penetration.

He should not speak ill of others,
Nor be given to rude or disrespectful conduct;
910c With a mind free of the desire for glory,
He should practise this meditation.

Honoring all the sutra-dharmas,
He should always delight in the Way;
With a mind free of insincerity and falseness,
He should eliminate mean and jealous thoughts.

He who studies this meditation
Should always behave respectfully;
Doing away with arrogance and self-indulgence,
He should serve the community of monks.

The bodhisattva Bhadrapāla said to the Buddha: "If a laywoman seeking to set out in the Mahayana should wish, when she hears this meditation, to study it and cultivate it, what dharmas should she practise to study and cultivate this meditation?"

The Buddha said to Bhadrapāla: "If a laywoman seeking to set out in the Mahayana should wish, when she hears this meditation, to study and cultivate it, she should keep the five precepts; she should commit herself to the three—what three? She should commit herself to the Buddha, commit her life to the Dharma, and commit her life to the community of monks—she should not follow other ways; she should not worship the gods; she should not take any notice of lucky days; she should not be flirtatious; she should not be unrestrained; and she should not have desires. The laywoman should always think of giving; she should wish eagerly to hear the sutras, and exert herself to increase her learning. The laywoman should always honor her good teachers; and she should always have an unremittingly attentive mind. If monks or nuns pass by, she should always give them hospitality by offering them a seat and waiting on them with food and drink."

The Buddha then recited the following verses:

If a laywoman
Recites this meditation,
She should follow the teachings of the Buddha's Dharma
And uphold the five precepts in their entirety.

When she cultivates this meditation,
She should honor the Buddha
As well as the Dharma and the community of monks,
And she should honor her good teacher.

She should not follow other ways,
She should not sacrifice to the gods;

Practising this meditation,
If she sees people she should rise and greet them.

She should give up killing, theft, and licentiousness,
She should be truthful and not two-tongued;
She should not go to wineshops;
She should practise this meditation.

Her mind should not harbor craving;
She should always think of giving;
She should do away with insincere thoughts,
And not talk about the shortcomings of others.

She should always honor and serve
Monks and nuns;
Hearing words of the Dharma she should accept them all;
Thus should she study the meditation.

Chapter VII

The Prediction

The bodhisattva Bhadrapāla asked the Buddha: "How wonderful that the God among Gods, the Tathāgata, has in this way preached this meditation, which all bodhisattvas delight in, practicing it energetically and not becoming slothful about supreme and perfect awakening. After the Buddha's Parinirvāṇa, will this meditation exist in Jambudvīpa?" 911a

The Buddha said to the bodhisattva Bhadrapāla: "After my Parinirvāṇa, this meditation will appear for forty years, after which it will no longer appear. Later, in the age of disorder, when the Buddha's sutras are about to vanish, the monks will no longer accept the Buddha's teachings. Afterward, in the age of disorder, state will take up arms against state. At that time this meditation will reappear in Jambudvīpa. Because of the Buddha's numinous power, this meditation sutra will again emerge."

The bodhisattva Bhadrapāla and the bodhisattva Ratnākara rose from their seats, put their robes in order, placed their hands together with interlacing fingers in front of the Buddha, and said to the Buddha: "After the Parinirvāṇa of the Buddha, in the age of disorder, we shall preserve this meditation together, keep this meditation, and preach it in full to others. We shall never tire of hearing the volumes of this sutra." Then the bodhisattva Mahāsusārthavāha, the bodhisattva Guhagupta, the bodhisattva Naradatta, the bodhisattva Susīma, the bodhisattva Indradatta, and the bodhisattva Varuṇadeva said to the Buddha: "When the Buddha has passed into Parinirvāṇa, later, in the age of disorder, together we shall personally preserve and keep the volumes of this sutra and perpetuate the Buddha's Way. If there are any who have not yet heard it, together we shall preach and teach it to them. We all accept this profound sutra, which few in the world believe." Then five hundred people rose from their seats. Monks and nuns, laymen and laywomen, they all placed their hands together with interlacing fingers, came before the Buddha, and said to the Buddha: "After the Buddha's Parinirvāṇa, in the age of disorder, when we hear this meditation we shall all personally keep it and preserve it. We would like you to entrust us five hundred people to these eight bodhisattvas."

Then the Buddha smiled, and a golden light shone from his mouth to the innumerable Buddha-fields of the ten quarters, illuminating them all brightly. Returning, it circled his body three times, and entered it through the top of his head. Ānanda rose from his seat, covered himself once again with his robe, and having come forward to where the Buddha was and made obeisance to the Buddha, he withdrew and remained with hands placed together with interlacing fingers, praising him with the following verses:

Your mind is pure, your conduct is immaculate,
Your divine powers of penetration are unlimited, you have great powers of magical transformation,
You have overcome all obstacles, your knowledge is extraordinary,
Your radiance dispels the darkness and removes defilement.

Your wisdom is incalculable, your mind entirely set free.
O Buddha, God among Gods, with the voice of the nightingale,
911b Whom none of the followers of other ways can disturb,
Why do you smile and emit this marvellous radiance?

I pray that the perfectly awakened one will explain it for us,
You who have love and compassion for all, Lord of beings,
If one hears the soft voice of the Buddha,

It explains how one advances to sagehood and changes
the ways of the world.

The Lord of the World does not show emotions for nothing,
The guide of all the sages does not smile in vain.
Who will now be given a prediction?
O Hero of the World, I pray that you explain the meaning
of this for us.

Who will this day be firmly established in the Way and
in virtue?
Who will succeed in setting out on the marvellous course?
Who will now receive the treasury of profound Dharmas,
The supreme Way and virtue to which all commit
themselves?

Who will this day have compassion for the world?
Who will take up this teaching of the Dharma?
Who will be firmly established in Buddha-wisdom?
Lord of the World, I pray that you explain this for us.

The Buddha then uttered the following verses to Ānanda:

The Buddha said: "Ānanda, do you see
The five hundred people standing before me
With joyful hearts, singing the words:
'We too shall obtain this Dharma'?

"With happy expressions on their faces, they regard the
Buddha respectfully:
'When shall we get to be like this?'
They all stand on tiptoes, praising the Buddha:
'We should certainly attain this.'

"Although the five hundred people now present
Have different names, their course of action has been the
same from the beginning;
They have always been happy to accept this profound sutra,
And will do so again in future ages.

"Now I charge you and announce to you:
The Buddha's knowledge, being incalculable, knows them from the beginning;
They have not just seen one Buddha,
Nor have they obtained their wisdom while standing here.

"Laid bare are their former lives,
During which they have seen eighty thousand Buddhas, one after the other;
The five hundred people kept to the Way,
Always understood the meaning of the sutras, and strove to realize it in practice.

"They urged on innumerable bodhisattvas,
Always practised love and compassion, and preserved the sutra-dharmas;
They encouraged and taught all the many people,
Bringing them all to the practice of the Great Way.

"They knew and saw past Lords of the World,
Saw eighty million billions of them;
Widely renowned, liberated in mind,
They preserved this Dharma which moves in three turns.

"Here, in the present age, they receive my teaching;
They will distribute and make offerings to these relics;
Calmly and carefully they will accept and study what the Buddha has taught,
They will all recite it and have their commission.

"They will place it in stupas and in the mountains,
Or they will entrust it to the gods, the dragons or the Gandharvas;
Each one, when he has handed over the volumes of the sutra,
Will at the end of his life be born in heaven above.

"When their lives in heaven above come to an end, they shall return to the world,
Each one being born of different stock.

They shall once more take up the practice of the Buddha's Way, 911c
And shall distribute this sutra in accordance with their vows.

"Because they love this sutra-dharma,
They will find it as soon as they look for it, take it and put it into practice.
They will cause innumerable people to hear it;
Their joy will be hard to measure, and their minds without equal.

"These wise ones will not tire of the Dharma;
They will not be attached to their persons or their lives;
They will vanquish all followers of heterodox ways;
They shall bestow the sutra-dharma and glorify its intent.

"Nobody can obtain, take up, recite
Or expound this sutra-dharma,
But the people of the four classes now standing in my presence,
The host of the five hundred are fit and able to take it up.

"These eight bodhisattvas—Bhadrapāla
Ratnākara, Naradatta,
Mahāsusārthavāha, Varuṇadeva,
Indradatta, Susīma, Guhagupta—

"The monks and nuns, and the pure believers
Accept the mysterious Dharma with its sentences of exalted meaning;
With the Way of the sutra they always show compassion to the world;
They proclaim widely the universal teaching that flows everywhere.

"The eight bodhisattvas—Bhadrapāla and the others—
Are the champions of the host of five hundred;
They will always take up the sutras of universality
And be free of attachment to the many ways of the world.

"Loosening all bonds, understanding the wisdom of emptiness,
With the color of polished red gold and the marks of a hundred blessings,
They constantly act with love and compassion, and deliver beings;
They dispense security and destroy all defilements.

"After their lives come to an end, they are born in families which uphold the Dharma;
They will never again return to the three evil destinies;
Following each other for generation after generation, they will always be in accord;
Afterward they shall attain the noble Way of the Buddha.

"They have already done away with the eight places of hardship,
And they avoid all the evil destinies;
No one can assess their meritorious conduct,
No one can measure the blessings they receive.

"They shall once more encounter the Buddha Maitreya,
And, being all of the same mind, will go to commit themselves to him;
Together they shall all make offerings, being of equal love and compassion;
They shall attain the sentence of supreme quiescence.

"Their minds are all in total harmony;
They intend rightly to serve the Lord among Men;
Not relying on worldly things, they will obtain patient acceptance of the Dharma,
And quickly attain the practice of the supreme Great Way.

"They shall always uphold this sutra-dharma,
Reciting it when they rise in the morning and retire in the evening,

They shall plant many merits and cultivate the holy life—
When they see Maitreya, such will their righteousness be.

"Under those Buddhas who arise in this Bhadrakalpa,
Radiating light out of love and compassion for the world,
Everywhere, wherever they are, they will take up the
Dharma,
And serve the Buddhas of the past, future, and present.

"They will all make offerings to the Heroes of the World;
Seeing the Lords of the Three Ages, they will be free of all
the poisons;
They shall quickly attain the noble Way of the Buddha,
Which is inconceivable and incalculable.

"Among them there are those who will attain the Way of 912a
the Buddha earlier;
The later ones will take turns in making offerings to them;
For countless aeons, numbering in the billions,
So they will go on until at last they come to an end.

"Here the laymen Bhadrapāla,
Ratnākara, Naradatta,
Susārthavāha, and Guhagupta
Have seen as many Buddhas as there are sands in the
Ganges.

"They shall always serve the teaching of the true Dharma
And propagate the Buddhas' teachings, uncountable even
by the million;
Their practice of the Way is incalculable, and could not be
measured,
Even over innumerable millions of aeons.

"Even if people were to take up their names
Wherever they were moving around, or in their dreams,
Such brave guides of the world as these
Would all attain the supreme Way.

"If those who, on seeing them or hearing their voices,
Are happy and joyful in their hearts
Will all doubtless attain the Way of the Buddha;
How much more so those who accept them and make offerings to them?

"If those who get angry with them and abuse them
Or strike them with evil intentions
Will, through the numinous power and grace of these eight men,
Be brought to Buddhahood nevertheless, how much more so those who honor them?

"The Dharmas which they have accepted are inconceivable;
Their names are incalculable, as are their life spans;
Their radiance is infinite, their virtues beyond doubt;
Their wisdom is incalculable, and so is their conduct.

"They always gain audience with incalculable Buddhas
Pure in the precepts, as numerous as the sands in the Ganges;
Under them they practise giving widely,
Thereby seeking the supreme Way.

"If one spoke of their blessings for innumerable millions of aeons,
One could not set a limit on their merit.
Those who accept this sutra-dharma, recite it and study it
Will have no further difficulty in attaining the Great Way.

"If anyone cherishes the volumes of this sutra
Accepts it, recites it, keeps it, and expounds it,
You should know that he is one of the five hundred people
Whose hearts cherish it, and never doubt it.

"If one is given this sutra-dharma,
Cherishes the message of the Way, and increases his energy,

Practises the pure precepts and eliminates sleepiness,
He will never have any difficulty in attaining this
meditation.

"Wishing to win ease and proclaim the sutras and the
precepts,
The monk takes up his studies in a solitary abode;
He always practises mendicancy and knows contentment;
He will never have any difficulty in attaining this
meditation.

"He avoids the noise of crowds and does not accept
invitations;
His mouth does not hanker after tastes, he has renounced
desires;
He honors as a Lord of the World with constant service
The person from whom he hears this sutra-dharma.

"Eliminating meanness, he accepts this Dharma;
He extirpates lust and renounces foolishness;
He sets out on the Great Way, and his mind is free of doubt;
Afterward he studies and practises this meditation.

"His conduct is unattached, he has rejected all desires;
He always shows self-restraint, and renounces anger
and hate;
Energetically he practises the teachings of the Buddha's 912b
Dharma;
Afterwards he accepts and studies this meditation.

"He does not covet sons and daughters or possessions;
He avoids arrogance and sets aside wives and concubines;
He who cultivates the Way living in the home always has
shame;
Afterward he studies and recites this meditation.

"He has no malicious thoughts, his behavior is gentle,
He takes no pleasure in abuse, rejecting all evil;

Not hunting after form, he obtains the patient acceptance
of the Dharma;
He should ably recite this meditation.

"If a nun studies this Dharma,
She should always be respectful and renounce arrogance;
She should avoid flirtatiousness and conceit,
And she will have no further difficulty in mastering this
meditation.

"Always acting energetically, eliminating sleepiness,
Without regard for self or regard for persons,
She who cherishes the Dharma does not begrudge her life;
Afterward she studies and recites this meditation.

"She checks licentiousness and abandons attachments,
Is free of angry thoughts and does away with insincerity;
She will never again fall into Māra's net;
Possessing this meditation, such are her attainments.

"She acts with equanimity towards all beings;
She eliminates self-indulgence and all the defilements;
She is not brusque by nature, nor coarse in her speech;
Afterward she studies and recites this meditation.

"She ought not to covet, even for a moment,
Bowls, robes, or clothes;
She should honor her good teachers, regarding them as
Buddhas;
Afterward she studies and recites this meditation.

"Securing thereby a fine advantage and avoiding the evil
destinies,
They single-mindedly believe and rejoice in the teachings
of the Buddha's Dharma,
And avoid all the eight places of hardship:
Such are the gains for those who keep this sutra."

Chapter VIII

Protection

The bodhisattva Bhadrapāla, the bodhisattva Ratnākara, the bodhisattva Guhagupta, the bodhisattva Naradatta, the bodhisattva Susīma, the bodhisattva Mahāsusārthavāha, the bodhisattva Indradatta, and the bodhisattva Varuṇadeva—when they heard what the Buddha said, these eight bodhisattvas all rejoiced greatly, and made offerings to the Buddha, presenting him with five hundred robes of Indian cotton and with precious gems, and committing themselves to him. The Buddha said to Ānanda: "This Bhadrapāla and his companions are the teachers of the five hundred bodhisattvas. Always upholding the central and true Dharma, they will come together and teach them as required, so that all will rejoice, having minds which are happy, minds which are adaptable, minds which are pure, and minds which reject desire." Then the five hundred all put their hands together with interlacing fingers and stood before the Buddha.

The bodhisattva Bhadrapāla said to the Buddha: "How many things should bodhisattvas possess to master this meditation, O God among Gods?" The Buddha said: "If bodhisattvas have four things they quickly master this meditation. What are the four? First, they have no faith in other ways. Second, they eradicate the
passions. Third, they act in accordance with the Dharma. Fourth, 912c
they have no desire for rebirth. These are the four, by which bodhisattvas quickly master this meditation."

The Buddha said to Bhadrapāla: "Any bodhisattvas who study this meditation, or keep it, or recite it, or cultivate it will obtain five hundred meritorious virtues for themselves in this very life. Bhadrapāla, it is like a monk with a loving heart—he is never harmed by poison, he is never harmed by weapons, fire cannot burn him, he cannot drown, and rulers cannot take advantage of him. In the same way, if bodhisattvas cultivate this meditation, they are never harmed by poison, never harmed by weapons, never burnt by fire, never drowned, and never taken advantage of by rulers. For example, Bhadrapāla, when the aeon is destroyed in flames, even if the bodhisattva who possesses this meditation were to fall into that fire, the fire would immediately be extinguished, in the same way that a large pitcher of water extinguishes a small fire."

The Buddha said to Bhadrapāla: "It is exactly as I say. As for those bodhisattvas who possess this meditation, if rulers or thieves or water or fire or dragons or snakes or Yakṣa spirits or wild beasts or pythons or flood-dragons or lions or tigers or wolves or dogs or humans or nonhumans or apes or hungry ghosts or Kumbhāṇḍa spirits try to molest people, or try to kill people, or try to rob people of their bowls and robes, or ruin people's meditation, or rob them of their mindfulness—if they wish to affect these bodhisattvas, they will never be able to do so." The Buddha said: "It is exactly as I say. Except for what they have brought on themselves in former lives, nothing else can affect them." The Buddha said: "It is exactly as I say. If bodhisattvas possess this meditation, they never suffer a sickness of the eyes; their ears, noses, mouths, and bodies are free of sickness; their minds never know grief or distress. If these bodhisattvas, when they are dying or are near death, should have these afflictions, things are not as the Buddha says—unless it be what they have done in former lives.

"Furthermore, Bhadrapāla, all the gods praise these bodhisattvas. All the dragons praise them. All the Yakṣa spirits praise them. All the Asuras praise them. All the Garuḍa spirits, Kinnara spirits, Mahoraga spirits, humans, and nonhumans praise these bodhisattvas. All the Buddhas, Gods among Gods, praise these bodhisattvas.

"Furthermore, Bhadrapāla, these bodhisattvas are protected by the gods, and are protected by the dragons. The Four Heavenly Kings, Śakra, Lord of the Gods, and the god Brahmā Sahāṃpati all protect these bodhisattvas. All the Yakṣa spirits, the Gandharva spirits, the Asura spirits, the Garuḍa spirits, the Kinnara spirits, the Mahoraga spirits, both humans and nonhumans together pro- 913a tect these bodhisattvas. All the Buddhas, Gods among Gods, together protect these bodhisattvas.

"Furthermore, Bhadrapāla, these bodhisattvas are held in high esteem by the gods. All the dragons, Yakṣa spirits, Gandharva spirits, Asura spirits, Garuḍa spirits, Kinnara spirits, Mahoraga spirits, humans, and nonhumans together hold these bodhisattvas in high esteem. The Buddhas, Gods among Gods, are all free of desire, yet on account of the Way and of virtue they all hold these bodhisattvas in high esteem.

"Furthermore, Bhadrapāla, all the gods wish to see these bodhisattvas. All the dragons, Yakṣa spirits, Gandharva spirits, Asura spirits, Garuḍa spirits, Kinnara spirits, Mahoraga spirits, humans, and nonhumans long for and wish to see these bodhisattvas. As for the Buddhas, the Gods among Gods, each and every one of them wishes to have these bodhisattvas go to him, he wishes to have them go for humanity's sake. Furthermore, Bhadrapāla, all the gods come to these bodhisattvas, all the dragons, Yakṣa spirits, Gandharva spirits, Asura spirits, Garuḍa spirits, Kinnara spirits, Mahoraga spirits, humans, and nonhumans come to these bodhisattvas, and they all see each other. As for the Buddhas, the Gods among Gods, the bodhisattvas not only see them during the daytime, but at night in their dreams they both see the Buddhas' bodies and each of the Buddhas tells them his own name.

"Furthermore, Bhadrapāla, as for sutras which these bodhisattvas have not hitherto recited and sutra volumes which they have not previously heard, these bodhisattvas will, by means of the numinous power of this meditation, obtain all the names of those sutra volumes in their dreams, they will see them all and hear all the sounds of the sutras. If they do not obtain them in the daytime, then they see and obtain them all at night in their dreams." The Buddha said to Bhadrapāla: "If for an aeon or for more than an aeon I were to proclaim the merits of these bodhisattvas who possess this meditation, I would not be able to come to an end, to say nothing of those who strive energetically to master this meditation."

The Buddha then recited the following verses:

Should any bodhisattvas study and recite this
Meditation expounded by the Buddha, with its message of quiescence,
Even if one wanted to praise their merits,
It would be like subtracting one grain of sand from the banks of the Ganges.

Knives and swords, spears and halberds do not wound them,
Robbers and foes cannot harm them,
Kings of states and great ministers look affectionately upon them:
Such are the results of studying this meditation.

If snakes which are poisonous and truly terrible
See those practitioners, their poison is quickly removed;
913b They no longer get angry or spit venom:
Such are the results of reciting this meditation.

Enemies who bear them ill-will are no match for them;
Gods, dragons, spirits, and Kinnaras
All fall silent when they see their numinous radiance;
Such are the results of studying this meditation.

Evil wolves and pythons of the wilds,
Lions, fierce tigers, deer, and apes,
Without harmful intentions, keeping their poison hidden,
All come to provide these practitioners with their personal protection.

Evil spirits who seize people's souls,
And all gods and human beings who harbor harmful intentions
Submit of their own accord when they sense their numinous power:
Such are the results of studying this meditation.

They do not fall sick, nor do they suffer pain;
Their hearing and vision are acute and clear, without
dimming or blockage;
Their eloquence in speaking is outstanding:
They who practise the meditation quickly attain this.

They never fall into hell,
And avoid the destiny of hungry ghosts and animals;
In all their rebirths, life after life, they remember their
former existences:
Such are the results of studying this meditation.

The spirits and Gandharvas together protect them,
As do the gods and human beings as well,
Along with the Asuras and the Mahoragas:
Such are the results of practicing this meditation.

All the gods together extol their virtues,
The gods, men, dragons, spirits, and Kinnaras;
The Buddhas praise them and fulfill their aspirations,
Because they recite the sutra and preach it for the
sake of others.

They do not regress in their aspiration to the Way,
Nor is the meaning of the Dharma wisdom exhausted
for them;
None can equal the beauty of their appearance,
If they recite and practise this sutra, and teach others.

When state takes up arms against state, and the people
are in turmoil,
When famine is rife, and there is dire need,
They never suffer an early death before their time is up,
They who can recite this sutra and teach others.

Valiantly they triumph over all the deeds of Māra;
Their minds know no fear, nor does their hair stand on end;
Their meritorious conduct is inconceivable:
Such are the results of practicing this meditation.

Bewitchery, magic, and the casting of spells,
The improper action of those who follow foul heretical ways,
Can never affect their persons,
Because they delight in the Dharma and know it thoroughly.

Everyone together sings of their virtues,
The honored sons of the Buddha, fully endowed with the knowledge of emptiness;
Such are the results for those into whose hands this sutra passes
Afterward, in the future, in the very last days.

They will always act energetically, and be joyful,
Will uphold this Dharma with one heart, harmoniously,
Will accept and keep the sutra volumes, expound and recite them;
It is therefore to them that I now speak.

Chapter IX

The Buddha Kṣemarāja

The Buddha said to Bhadrapāla: "Once upon a time, innumerable incalculable aeons ago, there was a Buddha by the name of Kṣemarāja, a Buddha, a Tathāgata, an Arhat, a Perfectly Awakened One, 913c
most highly honored in the world, a bringer of peace to the world, brilliant with regard to the sutras, and known as God among Gods in heaven and beneath it. At that time a certain elder's son by the name of Sudatta came with twenty thousand people to the Buddha Kṣemarāja, made obeisance to the Buddha, withdrew, and sat down to one side. The elder's son Sudatta asked the Buddha Kṣemarāja about this meditation. The Buddha Kṣemarāja, knowing what the elder's son Sudatta was thinking, then preached this meditation to him. When the elder's son Sudatta heard this meditation, he rejoiced greatly, and straightaway was able to recite and retain it all. He became an ascetic, and strove for this meditation for eighty thousand years, during which time the elder's son Sudatta heard a great many sutras from the Buddha. He heard sutras from innumerable Buddhas, and his wisdom was outstanding. Thereafter, when the life of the elder's son Sudatta came to an end, he was reborn in the heaven of the Gods of the Thirty-three. Subsequently, he came back down from heaven and was reborn in the world. At that time, in that ancient aeon, there was another Buddha by the name of Vidyuddeva, a Tathāgata, an Arhat, a Perfectly Awakened One. Then the Buddha had been born into a kṣatriya household. At that time the elder's son Sudatta once again heard this meditation under the Buddha, and once again strove for it. Then the elder's son Sudatta, later in that ancient aeon, met another Buddha by the name of Raṣmirāja, a Tathāgata,

an Arhat, a Perfectly Awakened One, of brahman stock. At that time the elder's son Sudatta again received this meditation under the Buddha, and strove to cultivate it for eighty-four thousand years." The Buddha said to Bhadrapāla: "Eighty thousand aeons later the elder's son Sudatta became a Buddha by the name of Dīpaṃkara. At that time the elder's son Sudatta was, as a man, brilliant and brave, and his wisdom was most extensive." The Buddha said: "Do you see this meditation, Bhadrapāla? Its abundant benefits are such that it causes people to realise the Way of the Buddha. Any bodhisattvas who attain this meditation should study and recite it, they should preserve it, they should teach it to others and they should cultivate it, and if they do this they will attain Buddhahood before long.

"Do you know, Bhadrapāla, that this meditation is the eye of bodhisattvas, is the mother of bodhisattvas, is the object of devotion of bodhisattvas, and is the origin of bodhisattvas? Do you know, Bhadrapāla, that this meditation destroys darkness, and illuminates everything above heaven and beneath it? Do you know, Bhadrapāla, that this bodhisattvas' meditation is the treasury of the Buddhas, is the ground of the Buddhas, is the fountainhead of the deep ocean of precious gems, is the stabilizer of incalculable meritorious virtues, the sutra which increases perspicacity? You
914a should know that this is what comes from the meditation. From within it emerges the Buddha and the hearing of the sutras.

"Establish yourself properly in the four stoppings of thought. What are the four stoppings of thought? First, one observes one's own body, and one observes the bodies of others; but when one observes one's own body and observes the bodies of others, there is from the beginning no body. Second, one observes one's own feelings, and one observes the feelings of others; but when one observes one's own feelings and observes the feelings of others, there are from the beginning no feelings. Third, one observes one's own thoughts and observes the thoughts of others, but when one observes one's own thoughts and observes the thoughts of others, there are from the beginning no thoughts. Fourth, one observes one's own dharmas and observes the dharmas of others, but when one observes one's own dharmas and observes the dharmas of others, there are from the beginning no dharmas."

The Buddha said to Bhadrapāla: "Who will believe in this meditation? The only people who will believe in it are the Tathāgatas, Arhats, and Perfectly Awakened Ones; those who do not regress; and arhats. Those with foolish and deluded minds are a long way from this Meditation in Which the Buddhas of the Present Stand Before One. Why? In this Dharma one should reflect on the Buddha and should see the Buddha." The Buddha said to Bhadrapāla: "These bodhisattvas should reflect on the Buddha, should see the Buddha, and should hear the sutras, but they should not have any attachment to them. Why? The Buddha is originally nonexistent, and these dharmas are uncaused. Why? They are originally empty and nonexistent. When each person undertakes reflection on dharmas, in these dharmas there is nothing to grasp, in these dharmas there is no attachment. They are like empty space; they are utterly pure. These dharmas are thought by people. They are completely nonexistent. They are nonexistent. These dharmas are apparent only; what is caused is merely empty and still like nirvana. These dharmas are nonexistent. Originally these dharmas do not exist; they come from nowhere and they go nowhere. People are originally nonexistent. Those unattached to these dharmas are close, while those who have attachments are far."

The Buddha said to Bhadrapāla: "Those who cultivate this meditation enter the formless by means of form; seeing the Buddha, they reflect on the Buddha and cultivate awakening; hearing the sutras, they reflect on the dharmas and cultivate awakening. They must not think of the self, and they must not become attached to the dharmas. Why? They are cultivating awakening. Bhadrapāla, there are those who cultivate awakening and do not see the Buddha. If they have so much as a hair of attachment they will not obtain the dharmas. If they give to others with expectations of something, that is not giving. If they keep the precepts with expectations of something, that is impurity. If they covet the

Dharma, they will not obtain nirvana. If they are insincere with regard to the sutras, they will not succeed in being brilliant. If they take pleasure in assemblies and delight in other ways, they will never be able to master the single practice. They whose thoughts run into difficulties when it comes to desire, and who get angry will not be capable of patient acceptance. They who hate will not succeed in preaching to others. They who are good at striving for the way of the arhats will not succeed here in seeing the Medita-
914b tion in Which the Buddhas of the Present All Stand Before One, and will not attain happiness in dharmas which do not come into existence, and establish themselves in it. They who have attachments will not master emptiness. Bodhisattvas must never be miserly. They who are slothful will not obtain the Way. They who are licentious will not enter into contemplation. They who have discursive thoughts will not enter into meditation."

The Buddha then recited the following verses:

Their merits are incalculable;
They uphold the precepts perfectly, and are unblemished;
Their minds are pure and devoid of defilement;
Such are the results of practicing this meditation.

Should any keep this meditation,
Their wisdom will be all-embracing and free of any
  deficiency;
They will comprehend all meanings and never forget
  anything;
Their meritorious conduct will be as bright as the moon.

Should any keep this meditation,
Their understanding and their aspiration to awakening
  will be inconceivable;
They will comprehend incalculable dharmas of the Way;
Innumerable gods will protect their virtue.

Should any keep this meditation,
They will always see innumerable Buddhas face to face,

And hear incalculable Buddhas expounding the Dharma,
Which they will immediately be able to retain, reflect on,
and practise widely.

Should any keep this meditation,
All evils and hardships will be done away with;
The Buddhas, who show compassion to the world,
Will all join in extolling these bodhisattvas.

If bodhisattvas should wish to see
Innumerable future Buddhas and Lords of the World,
Rejoice wholeheartedly, and take their stand in the true
Dharma,
They should study and recite this meditation.

Should any keep this meditation,
Their merits and blessings will be inconceivable;
They will be first and foremost in attaining a human body,
Preeminent in leaving the household and practicing
mendicancy.

Should any obtain this sutra at the very last,
They will attain the foremost merits and advantages;
They will obtain infinite blessings:
Such are the results of being established in this meditation.

Here Ends Fascicle Two
of The Pratyutpanna Samādhi Sutra

Fascicle Three

Chapter X

The Invitation to the Buddha

The bodhisattva Bhadrapāla put his robes in order, went down on his knees, placed his hands together with interlacing fingers, and said to the Buddha: "I wish to invite the Buddha and the community of monks to dinner tomorrow at my house; I would like the Buddha to accept the invitation out of compassion." The Buddha
and the community of monks all accepted the invitation in silence. 914c
The bodhisattva Bhadrapāla, knowing that the Buddha had accepted the invitation, rose and went to the nun Mahāprajāpatī, and said to her: "I would like you together with the nuns to accept my invitation to a modest meal tomorrow at my house." The nun Mahāprajāpatī then accepted the invitation. The bodhisattva Bhadrapāla said to the bodhisattva Ratnākara: "Younger brother, ask all the newcomers from all the states and provinces to assemble where the Buddha is." The bodhisattva Ratnākara came forward to the Buddha, made obeisance to him, went down on his knees, placed his hands together with interlacing fingers, and said to him: "My elder brother has invited the Buddha, and he wishes to invite all the newcomers to dinner at his house. I would like you to accept out of compassion."

The bodhisattva Bhadrapāla, the bodhisattva Ratnākara, the bodhisattva Guhagupta, the bodhisattva Naradatta, the bodhisattva Susīma, the bodhisattva Mahāsusārthavāha, the bodhisattva Indradatta, and the bodhisattva Varuṇadeva, all together with their relatives, came forward and touched the Buddha's feet with their foreheads, and made obeisance to the community of monks. When they had finished making obeisance they left the Buddha, returned to the city of Rājagṛha, and went to the house of the bodhisattva Bhadrapāla, where they helped each other prepare the food. The Four Heavenly Kings, Śakra, the Lord of the Gods, and Brahmā Sahāṃpati all came quickly to help the bodhisattva Bhadrapāla prepare all the food. Then the bodhisattva Bhadrapāla and his relatives together decorated the city of Rājagṛha. They covered the whole city with many different kinds of silk canopies, hung all its streets, lanes, and marketplaces with silk banners, and they scattered flowers and burned incense throughout the whole city. They prepared dishes of a hundred flavors for the Buddha, but the dishes for the community of monks, the nuns, the laymen and the laywomen, as well as for the impoverished beggars, were equally as pleasing. Why? Because they give impartially, and regard all people, as well as the species that flit and wriggle, as equal.

Bhadrapāla, the eight bodhisattvas, and their relatives went together to the Buddha at dinnertime, came forward, and touched the Buddha's feet with their foreheads, then withdrew and said to the Buddha: "The meal has all been prepared. We would like the Buddha to come." Then the Buddha and the community of monks all put on their robes, took up their bowls, and went together; while all those who had assembled there followed the Buddha into the city of Rājagṛha to the house of the bodhisattva Bhadrapāla.

The bodhisattva Bhadrapāla thought: "Now, through the Buddha's numinous power, let my house become extremely large and turn into beryl, so that those outside and those inside can see each other, so that those outside the city can all see inside my house, and those inside my house can see outside the city." The Buddha knew right away what Bhadrapāla was thinking. Thereupon the
915a Buddha displayed his numinous power and made Bhadrapāla's house extremely large; and all the people throughout the whole city could see inside the house.

The Buddha entered the house of the bodhisattva Bhadrapāla first and sat down. The community of monks, the nuns, the laymen and the laywomen, each in their separate groups, all sat down in the house. When the bodhisattva Bhadrapāla saw that the Buddha and the community of monks had sat down, he personally served the Buddha and the community of monks many hundred kinds of food, and poured the drinks with his own hand. When the Buddha and the monks, nuns, laymen, and laywomen had all finished eating, he gave the same to all the paupers, who were all equally satisfied. By means of the Buddha's numinous power and grace he satisfied them all. When the bodhisattva Bhadrapāla saw that the Buddha and the disciples had all eaten, he came forward with water for washing, and finally took a small bench and sat down in front of the Buddha to listen to the sutras.

The Buddha expounded the sutras to the bodhisattva Bhadrapāla and the four classes of disciples, and everyone rejoiced, everyone enjoyed listening, everyone wanted to listen. The Buddha engaged the community of monks and all the disciples with the sutras. The Buddha rose and departed with the community of monks.

When the bodhisattva Bhadrapāla had eaten, he left the city of Rājagṛha with his relatives and went to the Buddha. Having come forward they made obeisance to the Buddha. They withdrew and sat down on one side, together with the bodhisattva Ratnākara, the bodhisattva Guhagupta, the bodhisattva Naradatta, the bodhisattva Susīma, the bodhisattva Mahāsusārthavāha, the bodhisattva Indradatta, and the bodhisattva Varuṇadeva. The bodhisattva Bhadrapāla, seeing that the multitude were all seated comfortably, came forward and asked the Buddha: "How many things does it take for bodhisattvas to attain the Meditation in Which the Buddhas of the Present All Stand Before One?"

The Buddha said to the bodhisattva Bhadrapāla: "If bodhisattvas possess five things, they quickly obtain the Meditation in Which the Buddhas of the Present All Stand Before One, study it, preserve it, and carefully practise it with a mind which does not turn back. What are the five? First, they find happiness in the profound sutras which are forever inexhaustible, which are infinite, which deliver one from all disasters, whereby one is freed from all defilements, whereby one leaves the darkness, enters the light, in which all

obscurities are eliminated." The Buddha said to Bhadrapāla: "If these bodhisattvas succeed in finding happiness in dharmas which do not come into existence from anywhere, they master this meditation. Furthermore, Bhadrapāla, they find no further happiness in places where one goes to be reborn: this is the second. They find no further happiness in other ways: this is the third. They find no further happiness in the passions: this is the fourth. They control themselves and practise the infinites: this is the fifth. If the bodhisattvas possess a further five things they quickly master this meditation. What are the five? First, in giving, their hearts should be free of regret; they should not crave anything or begrudge anything. Because of this they should not have any expectations. After they
915b have given to others they should never regret it. Furthermore, Bhadrapāla, the bodhisattvas give the gift of the sutras; they preach the sutras to other people; their speech is calm and careful, it is free of impediments, and they begrudge nothing. They preach the profound word of the Buddha, which they themselves practise and in which they establish themselves. Furthermore, Bhadrapāla, the bodhisattvas are not envious, have no doubt about what they do, eliminate sleepiness, eliminate the five desires, do not speak of their own good points, and do not speak ill of other people. If anyone reviles them, or if anyone belittles them, they should not get angry, nor should they become resentful, nor should they become remiss. Why? Because they have embarked upon the practice of emptiness. Furthermore, Bhadrapāla, the bodhisattvas set themselves to study this meditation and also teach it to other people. They copy this sutra, writing it on a fine length of plain silk, and perpetuate it. Furthermore, Bhadrapāla, the bodhisattvas' faith is considerable. They like and respect their elders and friends. With new students, if they receive a gift they should think of repaying the favor. They always have discerning faith. When they receive a small gift from another, they think of repaying it with a larger one; how much more so when it is considerable? The bodhisattvas always delight in and respect the sutras; they discard the meanings that are not to be repeated and they always reflect on those that are to be repeated. If they are like this they master the meditation quickly."

The Buddha then recited the following verses:

They always love the Dharma, abide in deep understanding,
Do not crave rebirth among any of the habitual desires,
And range through the five destinies without any attachments;
They who practise in this way will master the meditation.

They delight in giving without any thought of recompense;
In showing kindness they are free of attachment, and do not give it a second thought;
In giving, they are unaware that there is any recipient;
They only wish to understand the Buddha's profound knowledge.

Out of pity for beings they undertake giving;
Their hearts rejoice, and they have no regrets;
They are always established in giving, the precepts, patient acceptance,
Energy, singlemindedness and wisdom.

Fully endowed with the six transcendences, [the means of] attracting everyone,
And the four states of equanimity of love, compassion, joy, and circumspection,
Adept in the use of expedients, delivering beings;
They who practise in this way will master the meditation.

They who undertake giving and eliminate miserliness
Give with a joyful heart,
And, after they have given, remain ever joyful;
They who practise in this way will master the meditation.

They understand the sutra-dharmas and analyze their phrases,
They listen to the profound and essential message taught by the Buddha;
They expound the teaching of the wondrous Way and of Virtue;
They who practise in this way will master the meditation.

They study and recite this meditation;
Fully endowed with understanding, they preach it to others;
They ensure that this sutra-dharma is perpetuated;
They who practise in this way will master the meditation.

They never make a secret of the Buddha's sutra-dharma;
They expound it without expecting offerings;
915c They only seek the peaceful state of the Buddha's Way;
They who practise in this way will master the meditation.

They eliminate attachments and discard all obstacles;
They get rid of arrogance and pride;
They do not praise themselves or talk about the shortcomings of others;
They never again give rise to the thought of "I" and "me."

If they possess quiescence, thoughts do not arise;
Then they are able to understand the wisdom of this concentration of the Way;
They discard insincerity, and their minds are pure;
Therefore they quickly attain the patient acceptance of non-origination.

They always conduct themselves with the utmost honesty, open and unadorned;
They fulfill their vows entirely, without any defect;
They increase all the true virtues, and do no evil deed;
They who love the Dharma quickly attain the Way.

They never forget the sutras that they have recited;
They always preserve the precepts and purity of conduct;
They who practise in this way quickly attain Buddhahood,
To say nothing of obtaining this calm meditation.

The Buddha said to the bodhisattva Bhadrapāla: "Formerly, innumerable aeons ago, during the time of the Buddha Dīpaṃkara, I heard this meditation in the presence of the Buddha Dīpaṃkara, and immediately took it up. I saw the innumerable Buddhas of the ten quarters, heard the sutras from all of them and retained them all. Then all the Buddhas said to me: 'Innumerable aeons hereafter you shall become a Buddha by the name of Śākyamuni.'" The Buddha said to the bodhisattva Bhadrapāla: "Therefore I say to you: you yourself shall now attain Buddhahood. You should study this meditation in order to know the inner Dharma, which is foremost, which is beyond the reach of the masses, which leaves behind all forms. Any who establish themselves in this meditation will by reflection attain the Way of the Buddha."

The Buddha then recited the following verses:

> I remember that long ago, in the time of the Buddha
> Dīpaṃkara,
> I obtained this meditation;
> Then I saw the innumerable Buddhas of the ten quarters
> And heard them preach the profound and subtle message
> of the noble Dharma.
>
> Just as a man of virtue goes to gather gems
> And straightaway gets what he hopes for, according to
> his wish,
> So too the bodhisattva, the great man,
> Seeks gems in the sutras and then attains Buddhahood.

The bodhisattva Bhadrapāla said to the Buddha: "God among Gods, how should people cultivate this meditation?" The Buddha said to the bodhisattva Bhadrapāla: "They should not be attached to form. They should not have any inclinations towards rebirth. They should practise emptiness. They should cultivate this meditation. What is the meditation? It is that which one should practise in accordance with these dharmas. Furthermore, Bhadrapāla, when the bodhisattvas contemplate their own body, they have no body, nor do they contemplate anything, nor do they see anything, nor do they become attached to anything. Yet from the beginning they are not blind to anything, nor are they deaf to anything. As with the dharmas in the sutras, they continue to observe them, but they see nothing, nor do they become attached to anything. They

who have no attachments are those who cultivate the Way. They
916a have no doubts with regard to the dharmas. They who do not doubt see the Buddhas. They who see the Buddhas have their doubts cut off. The dharmas do not come into existence from anywhere. Why? If bodhisattvas have a doubting thought with regard to the dharmas, then that is attachment. What is attachment? That there are for them persons, there are lives, there are virtues, there are the dark ones [the aggregates], there are the entrances [the sense-fields], there are the objects [the elements], there are forms, there are the bases [of cognition], there are desires—this is attachment. Why? If bodhisattvas see the dharmas, they have no attachments, they neither think of nor see these dharmas. In what way do they not see? Bodhisattvas do not see in the same way as, for example, a stupid person studying another way, who maintains there is a self because there is for him a person. In what way do bodhisattvas see? Just as, for example, the Tathāgatas, Arhats and Perfectly Awakened Ones, those who do not regress, the pratyekabuddhas and the arhats are not happy or sad at what they see, so too bodhisattvas see without becoming happy or sad. They who cultivate this meditation are neither happy nor sad. Just as empty space is formless, featureless, pure, and unblemished, so do bodhisattvas see the dharmas. With unobstructed vision they see the dharmas. Therefore they see the Buddhas. They see the Buddhas as being like a bright moon-pearl set on beryl; like the sun when it has just risen; like the moon on the fifteenth day amidst all the stars; like a universal monarch with all his ministers in attendance; like the King of the Heaven of the Thirty-three, Śakra, Lord of the Gods, among all the gods; like Brahmā, King of the Gods, enthroned on high among all the Brahmā gods; like a torch blazing on the summit of a high mountain; like the King of Physicians healing the illnesses of people with medicines; like a lion going his solitary way; like all the wild geese flying through the air, with their leader out in front; like the piled snow on a high mountain under the winter moon, clearly visible on all four sides; like the Adamantine Mountains, the great boundary of heaven and earth, warding off

impurity; like the nether waters which support the earth; like the winds which support the water, purified of all defilements, the same as empty space; like the summit of Mount Sumeru, adorned with the Heaven of the Thirty-three. Such are the Buddhas. The Buddhas' observance of the precepts, the Buddhas' numinous power, and the Buddhas' meritorious virtues shine most brightly in innumerable realms. In this way do these bodhisattvas see the Buddhas of the ten quarters, hear the sutras, and accept them all."

The Buddha then recited the following verses:

The Buddhas are immaculate and undefiled;
With their host of meritorious virtues they are quite free of attachments;
Exalted their powers of numinous penetration, and marvellous their voices;
With the drum of the Dharma they convey the meaning and teach all the sounds.

Make offerings of all kinds of fragrant flowers
To the awakened Gods among Gods, liberated in wisdom;
With innumerable virtues present the relics 916b
With banners, canopies, and perfumes, in search of the meditation.

Hear the all-marvellous Dharma and master it completely;
Avoid downfall and understand quiescence;
Never think discursively of, or become attached to, empty dharmas;
You should aim at understanding profound and unobstructed knowledge.

Pure like the moon or the sun radiating light,
Resembling the god Brahmā in his original palace—
Call to mind the Lords of the World with a mind that is always pure,
In your thoughts be free of attachment, not thinking discursively of emptiness.

Like the winter moon or snow in the high mountains,
Or like the king of a state, a lord among men,
Or the pure pearl, which surpasses all gems—
So should you contemplate the Buddhas' marks and characteristics.

Like the kings of geese in flight with a leader out in front,
Or space which is pure and undefiled,
So too are the Buddhas, whose color is that of polished red gold;
The Buddha's sons, reflecting on them, make offerings to the Lords.

Eliminate all obscurities, get rid of dimness,
And then you shall quickly attain the pure meditation;
Discard all thoughts and wishes;
With immaculate conduct you shall obtain mental concentration.

Be undefiled, free yourself of impurity,
Get rid of anger and be without stupidity;
If one's vision is clear and naturally bright,
One will encounter no obstruction in calling to mind the Buddhas' meritorious virtues.

If one ponders the moral purity of the Buddhas, the Lords of the World,
One's mind is free of attachment and does not long for anything;
One does not see 'I' or 'me' or possessions,
Nor is there any arising in forms and signs.

If one discards birth-and-death and is free of all views,
Gets rid of arrogance and is pure in knowledge,
Avoids haughtiness and is not conceited,
One hears the tranquil meditation and avoids wrong views.

If any monk, son, or grandson of the Buddha,
Or faithful nun, or man of pure faith,
Or woman of pure faith who has done away with desire
Should reflect on it or energetically study it, they will
master this Dharma.

Chapter XI

Formlessness

The Buddha said to the bodhisattva Bhadrapāla: "Any bodhisattvas who wish to study this meditation and quickly master it, should first eliminate any conception of form, and should get rid of conceit. When they have eliminated conceptions and when they are no longer conceited, then they should study this meditation, and they should not be disputatious. What is disputatiousness? It is slandering emptiness. Therefore, they should not join in disputes, and they should not slander emptiness, and then they should recite this meditation."

The Buddha said to Bhadrapāla: "For any bodhisattvas who study and recite this meditation, there are ten things in which they should establish themselves. What are the ten? First, if any other people are presented with bowls, robes, or clothes they are not envious. Second, they should love and respect others and show filial obedience to their seniors. Third, they should repeatedly think
of repaying favors. Fourth, they do not speak falsely and avoid 916c
what is contrary to the Dharma. Fifth, they always practise mendicancy and do not accept invitations. Sixth, they should be energetic in walking up and down. Seventh, they should not go to sleep by day or by night. Eighth, they always wish to give gifts to the whole wide world, without begrudging anything or ever having regrets. Ninth, they immerse themselves deeply in wisdom and are without attachments. Tenth, they should first honor and serve their good teachers and regard them as Buddhas, and only then should they recite this meditation. These are the ten things.

"They should accord with Dharma, and then they who act in this way will obtain eight things. What are the eight things? First, they are pure in the precepts to the very last detail. Second, they do not have anything to do with other ways, and move in wisdom. Third, they are pure in wisdom, and have no further craving for rebirth. Fourth, their vision is pure, and they no longer desire birth-and-death. Fifth, they are highly learned, and free of attachment. Sixth, they are pure in energy, and realise the attainment of Buddhahood for themselves. Seventh, if anyone makes offerings to them, they are not happy because of it. Eighth, they are truly set on supreme and perfect awakening and are not to be swayed from it. These are the eight things."

The Buddha then recited the following verses:

> Those who possess wisdom do not give rise to conceptions,
> They eliminate conceit and arrogance,
> Always practise patient acceptance, and are not negligent;
> Only then should they study this meditation.
>
> Wise people have clear minds, and do not take issue with emptiness,
> Signlessness and quiescence, which is nirvana;
> They do not slander the Dharma or take issue with the Buddha;
> They who practise in this way master the meditation.
>
> Intelligent people are not conceited about this;
> They are ever mindful of the grace of the Buddha, and of the teacher of Dharma;
> They are firmly established in pure faith, and their determination does not waver;
> Only then should they study this meditation.
>
> In their hearts they do not harbor envy, and they avoid dimness;
> They do not have doubts but always have faith;
> They should practise energetically, without getting lazy;
> They who practise in this way master the meditation.
>
> Monks who study this always practise mendicancy,
> And do not accept invitations or go to gatherings;

There is no attachment in their hearts, and they do not amass anything;
They who practise in this way master the meditation.

If this Dharma teaching comes into people's hands
And they preserve and practise this sutra-text,
Wholeheartedly treat them like Buddhas;
Afterward study and recite this meditation.

Abiding in this supreme virtue and practising sincere faith,
They who would study and recite the meditation
Will speedily attain these eight dharmas,
Which are pure and immaculate, and taught by the Buddhas.

Their purity in the precepts will be thorough,
Their meditation will be flawless, and they will obtain similar views;
They regard birth-and-death as empty and pure;
Established in this Dharma they will attain perfection.

Their wisdom is pure and free of excess, 917a
Nor do those of undefiled conduct become attached;
They have wide learning and deep knowledge but refrain from squandering it;
They who succeed in practising in this way are wise.

Those who are determined and energetic do not suffer loss;
They do not crave offerings or gain;
They quickly attain the supreme Way of Buddhahood;
They who study such virtues as these have bright knowledge.

Chapter XII

The Eighteen Exclusives and the Ten Powers

The Buddha said: "They who obtain the above eight things will then acquire eighteen things proper to a Buddha. What are the eighteen things? First, on such-and-such a day he attains Buddhahood, and on such-and-such a day he enters Parinirvāṇa; from the day he first attains Buddhahood until the day of the Parinirvāṇa, the Buddha does not suffer any difficulties. Second, he has no shortcomings. Third, he does not forget anything. Fourth, he never loses his composure. Fifth, he never has the conception of a dharma or uses the word 'mine.' Sixth, he is never incapable of accepting things patiently. Seventh, he never lacks joy. Eighth, he never lacks energy. Ninth, he is never unreflecting. Tenth, he is never out of meditation. Eleventh, he never lacks knowledge. Twelfth, he never lacks liberated insight and knowledge. Thirteenth, with regard to the events of innumerable past ages, there is never anything that can stop the Buddha's unobstructed insight and knowledge. Fourteenth, with regard to the events of innumerable future ages there is never anything that can stop the Buddha's unobstructed insight and knowledge. Fifteenth, with regard to the events of innumerable ages now, at present, in all the ten quarters, there is never anything that can stop the Buddha's unobstructed insight and knowledge. Sixteenth, the acts which his body performs have their source in wisdom and are always accompanied by wisdom. Seventeenth, the utterances which his mouth makes have their source in wisdom and are always accompanied by wisdom. Eighteenth, the thoughts which his mind thinks have their source in wisdom and are always accompanied by wisdom. Those are the eighteen things proper to a Buddha."

The Buddha said to Bhadrapāla: "There are ten dharmas which preserve any bodhisattvas who are no longer subject to attachment, who seek the Dharma and preserve and study this meditation in its entirety. What are the ten dharmas which preserve? The ten powers of a Buddha. What are the ten powers? First, he knows fully the finite and the infinite. Second, from first to last he knows everything about the past, future, and present. Third, he knows fully the purity of emancipations and concentrations. Fourth, he knows all the various types of faculties and energy and the different thoughts of others. Fifth, he knows all the various kinds of faith. Sixth, he knows all the innumerable events caused by the many kinds of transformation. Seventh, he understands all, comprehends all, and knows all. Eighth, he knows all, his vision being unobstructed. Ninth, he knows all from first to last, without limit. Tenth, he
917b regards past, future, and present as all the same, and has no preferences or attachments." The Buddha said to Bhadrapāla: "If any bodhisattvas preserve all the dharmas which do not originate from anywhere, those bodhisattvas obtain the ten powers of a Buddha."

The Buddha then recited the following verse:

> The eighteen exclusive dharmas of the fully awakened one
> And the powers of the Lord of the World, of which there
> are now ten—
> If one takes up the practice of this meditation
> One will speedily attain them. It will never take long.

Chapter XIII

Encouragement

The Buddha said to Bhadrapāla: "These bodhisattvas possess four things which help them to rejoice[7] over this meditation: 'The Buddhas of the past who rejoiced over this meditation and studied this sutra, achieved for themselves full awakening to supreme and perfect awakening, and became fully endowed with knowledge. In the same way I shall rejoice.' Furthermore, Bhadrapāla: 'Future Buddhas pursuing the Way of the bodhisattva who rejoice over this meditation and study this meditation shall achieve for themselves full awakening to supreme and perfect awakening, and become fully endowed with knowledge.' They all rejoice in this way. Furthermore, Bhadrapāla: 'The innumerable Buddhas of the present, in all the ten quarters, who, when they originally pursued the way of the bodhisattva, rejoiced over this meditation and studied this meditation, have achieved for themselves full awakening to supreme and perfect awakening, and have become fully endowed with knowledge.' 'All those blessings from rejoicing, let them be shared with all the people of the ten quarters down to the species that flit and wriggle, so that full awakening to supreme and perfect awakening may be attained! By means of this merit from rejoicing over this meditation let them quickly master this meditation and succeed in becoming fully awakened to supreme and perfect awakening before long!'"

The Buddha said to Bhadrapāla: "As for the merit of these bodhisattvas which is connected with the four aspects of rejoicing over this meditation, I shall give a small illustration of it. It is like a man whose life lasts a hundred years, who, from the moment he is born, walks for a hundred years without ever resting. That man's pace exceeds that of a swift wind, and he goes around the four quarters,

the zenith, and the nadir. What would you say, Bhadrapāla? Would anybody be able to calculate that distance?" Bhadrapāla said: "Nobody could calculate that distance, God among Gods, except for the Buddha, the disciple Śāriputra, and non-regressing bodhisattvas—they are the only ones who could calculate it." The Buddha said to Bhadrapāla: "Therefore I say to all bodhisattvas: if any good man or good woman were to take these realms in the four quarters, the zenith, and the nadir, the places where that man has gone, and fill them with precious gems and make an
917c offering of them to the Buddha, that would not be as good as hearing this meditation. If any bodhisattvas hear this meditation and rejoice over these four matters, their blessings exceed those of him who makes an offering to the Buddha a hundred times over, a thousand times over, ten thousand times over, a million times over. Do you see, Bhadrapāla? Are the blessings of these bodhisattvas who rejoice not considerable? Therefore you should know: the blessings of these bodhisattvas who rejoice are extremely great."

The Buddha then recited the following verses:

With regard to the teaching of this sutra
They possess the four matters for rejoicing,
All the past, the future,
And the present Lords of the World.

The meritorious conduct of encouragement
Liberates all the ten quarters;
Even those things that flit and wriggle
All attain equal awakening.

If, for example, all around here,
In the four quarters, the zenith, and the nadir
A man, once born, were to walk for a hundred years,
Walk without stopping until the end of his life;

Should one want to measure the distance,
Its extent would be hard to calculate:
Only the Buddha and his disciple would know,
As well as non-regressing bodhisattvas.

To fill it with precious gems and give them
Would not be as good as hearing this Dharma.
As for the four matters for encouragement,
Their blessings surpass that.

Bhadrapāla, for the time being observe these
Four matters for rejoicing;
Giving, multiplied by myriads of millions,
Is not equal to encouragement.

Chapter XIV

The Buddha Siṃhamati

The Buddha then said to Bhadrapāla, "Long ago, in the distant past, in a time incalculable aeons ago, incalculable beyond reckoning, beyond number, beyond measure, beyond limit, at that time there was a Buddha by the name of Siṃhamati, a Tathāgata, an Arhat, a Perfectly Awakened One, of unequalled numinous power, bringer of peace to the world, lord of the sutras, and known as God among Gods in heaven and beneath it. Among the deserted places of this world, this realm of Jambudvīpa was fertile, thickly peopled, and happy. At that time Jambudvīpa extended eighteen myriad million billion leagues from north to south and east to west. At that time there were in Jambudvīpa altogether six hundred and forty myriad city-states. At that time in Jambudvīpa there was a great city-state by the name of Bhadraṃkara, and in this city-state were sixty million people. The Buddha Siṃhamati lived in this city-state. A certain universal monarch by the name of King Viśeṣagāmin went to the Buddha Siṃhamati, made obeisance to 918a
the Buddha, withdrew and sat down on one side. Then the Buddha Siṃhamati, knowing straightaway what that king was thinking, preached this meditation to him. Hearing this meditation, that king rejoiced, and then he sprinkled precious gems over the Buddha, and in his heart he thought: 'By virtue of this merit may all the people of the ten quarters be set at ease!' Then, following the Parinirvāṇa of the Buddha Siṃhamati, the universal monarch Viśeṣagāmin was, after his life had come to an end, reborn in a royal household, where he became a crown prince by the name of Brahmadatta. At that time there was in Jambudvīpa a highly learned monk by the name of Ratna, who then preached this meditation to the four groups of disciples—monks, nuns, laymen, and

laywomen. When the crown-prince Brahmadatta heard this meditation, he rejoiced; in his heart he was elated and overjoyed to hear this sutra, and he sprinkled precious gems worth hundreds of millions over this monk, and in addition made him offerings of fine robes; and thereby he conceived the intention of seeking the Way of the Buddha. Then, along with a thousand people, he shaved his head and beard and became an ascetic under this monk; and then, under this monk, he sought to learn this meditation from him. Together with the thousand monks, he served his teacher unremittingly for eight thousand years; from first to last, only once did he get to hear this meditation. On hearing this meditation, this group of monks rejoiced over the four matters, and assumed the wisdom of great learning. Thereafter, by virtue of the merit from this rejoicing, [Brahmadatta] saw sixty-eight thousand Buddhas one after the other, and each time, under each and every Buddha, he heard this meditation, which he cultivated and studied himself and taught other people how to study as well. By virtue of the merit of this rejoicing, that man afterward became a Buddha, a Tathāgata, an Arhat, and a Perfectly Awakened One by the name of Dṛḍhavīrya. Then the thousand monks subsequently attained full awakening to supreme and perfect awakening, all of them becoming Tathāgatas, Arhats, and Perfectly Awakened Ones by the name of Dṛḍhaśūra, and they taught countless people to seek the Way of the Buddha."

The Buddha said to Bhadrapāla: "What person, hearing this meditation, would not rejoice over it? What person would not study it? What person would not preach it to other people? What person would not cultivate it?" The Buddha said to Bhadrapāla: "Any bodhisattvas who cultivate this meditation shall quickly attain Buddhahood. Bhadrapāla, any bodhisattvas who hear of the existence of someone who possesses this meditation at a distance of twenty kilometers should, once they hear of him, immediately go in search of him, and make their way to where he is. If they only get to hear of someone who knows of the existence of this meditation,
918b they should always seek him out; so how much more should they do so if they get to hear of someone who is studying it? If they hear

of the existence of someone who possesses this meditation fifty kilometers away, or two thousand kilometers distant, they should go to where he is to study it, having merely got to hear of someone who knows it; so how much more should they do so if they get to hear of someone who is studying it?" The Buddha said: "If it is far away they should still always go in search of it, so how much more should they not go to look for it and study it if they hear that there is someone who possesses this meditation five or ten kilometers away?

"Bhadrapāla, any bodhisattvas who, hearing of this meditation, wish to go to that place and hear and strive for this meditation, should serve their teachers for ten years or one hundred years, they should make them offerings and venerate them totally. These bodhisattvas should not be self-serving, but should follow their teachers' teaching. They should always be grateful to their teachers." The Buddha said: "Therefore I tell you this: if, when bodhisattvas hear that this meditation is to be found two thousand kilometers away, they wish to go there, then, even if they do not succeed in hearing this meditation," the Buddha said, "I tell you that those people, because they had the energy to go in search of it, will never again lose the Way of the Buddha, and will certainly realise Buddhahood for themselves. Do you see, Bhadrapāla? Bodhisattvas who hear of this meditation and want to strive for it unremittingly obtain a most exalted benefit."

The Buddha then recited the following verses:

> I remember that in the past there was a Tathāgata,
> A Lord among Men called Siṃhamati.
> At that time there was a king, a ruler of men,
> Who went to that Buddha and heard the meditation.
>
> Intently and wisely he listened to this sutra;
> With incalculable joy in his heart he accepted the Dharma;
> Then he sprinkled precious gems over him
> And made offerings to Siṃhamati, Lord among Men.
>
> The thought came to him, and he exclaimed:
> 'Here, at a future time, I myself

Will uphold the Buddha's teaching, not daring to violate it,
And I shall attain this meditation!'

Because of this meritorious vow, after his life had come to an end,
He returned straightaway and was reborn in a royal household.
Then he saw the noble monk
By the name of Ratna, whose wisdom was all-embracing.

At the proper time he heard this meditation from him;
Elated, he rejoiced and accepted it,
And made offerings to him of many millions of fine things,
Precious gems and marvellous robes, for the sake of the Way.

Then with a thousand people he removed his hair and beard,
Resolutely aspiring to this meditation;
Simultaneously, for a full eight thousand years,
They followed the monk constantly, and did not forsake him.

They succeeded in hearing it once, not twice,
This meditation which is like the sea.
Holding the volumes of the sutra they recited and preached it;
Wherever they were born, they heard the meditation.

Because they had accumulated this merit,
They always saw the Buddhas, those of great numinous power;
918c Throughout that full eighty thousand years,
Whenever they saw the Buddhas, they made offerings to them.

They encountered sixty thousand million Buddhas,
And in addition made offerings to six thousand Lords;

Hearing the Dharma they preached, they rejoiced greatly;
Afterward they saw the Buddha Siṃhamati.

Receiving this merit [Brahmadatta] was reborn in a royal household,
And saw the Buddha by the name of Dṛḍhavīrya,
Who taught countless millions of people,
And delivered all from the afflictions of birth-and-death.

After reciting and studying this Dharma
He then also saw the Buddha named Dṛḍhaśūra,
Whose praises were sung in heaven above and in the world;
Merely by hearing the sound of the meditation he attained Buddhahood—

How much more then, those who accept it, recite it, or preach it,
Free of attachment in all the worlds,
Who propagate and distribute this meditation
Without ever doubting or forgetting the Way of the Buddha?

This meditation sutra is truly the word of the Buddha.
If one hears that this sutra is to be found in a distant place,
One should go to hear it and receive it, for the sake of the Dharma of the Way,
One should recite it single-mindedly, and not let it slip away.

Even if people go in search of it, but do not get to hear it,
Their merit and blessings will be inexhaustible;
No one could assess their virtue and righteousness,
Much less theirs, who do hear it and take it up.

Any who aspire to this meditation
Should recall that Brahmadatta of old.
Teach and uphold it, and never turn back:
This is what the monk who obtains the sutra should do.

Chapter XV

The Buddha Satyanāma

The Buddha said: "Long ago in the past there was another Buddha by the name of Satyanāma, a Tathāgata, an Arhat, and a Perfectly Awakened One. At that time there was a monk by the name of Varuṇa. After the Parinirvāṇa of that Buddha, this monk was in possession of this meditation. I was then a king of the kṣatriya caste, and in a dream I heard about this meditation. On waking, I then went in search of the monk who possessed this meditation, and forthwith became an ascetic under him. I wished to hear this meditation once under this monk. I served the teacher for thirty-six thousand years, but because of the frequent occurrence of acts of Māra I did not once succeed in hearing it."

The Buddha said to the monks, nuns, laymen, and laywomen: "Therefore I say to you: you should quickly accept this meditation, and you should not forget it. You should serve your teacher well and take up this meditation. Whether it takes one aeon or a hundred aeons or a thousand aeons, you should not grow lazy. You should master this meditation at once. Look after your good teacher and do not forsake him. Present the teacher with food and drink, with goods, with clothes, with beds and bedding, with a thousand myriad precious gems; make offerings to the teacher without begrudging anything. If you have nothing, you should go and beg for food, and offer it to the teacher. You should master this meditation at once, and not tire of it." The Buddha said: "Setting aside 919a
these offerings, which are just not worth mentioning, you should always cut off your own flesh and offer it to the good teacher, you should never begrudge him your person, how much less anything

else? You should serve the good teacher as a slave serves his lord. Those people who seek this meditation should know this. Having mastered this meditation they should hold fast to it, and always be grateful to their teachers." The Buddha said: "This meditation is difficult to meet with. Even if one sought this meditation for a hundred million aeons and only wished to hear its name, one might not be able to hear it, much less study it or teach it to others in one's turn. If one filled with precious gems as many Buddha-fields as there are grains of sand on the banks of the Ganges and made a gift of them, wouldn't the blessings from that be considerable? Yet that would not compare with copying this meditation or preserving the volumes of the sutra, the blessings from which would be extensive beyond computation."

The Buddha then recited the following verses:

I myself remember how, in a past age,
For years whose number reached a full sixty thousand,
I always followed a teacher of the Dharma, without
forsaking him,
Yet from the first I did not succeed in hearing this
meditation.

There was a Buddha whose name was Satyanāma,
Who then knew a monk called Varuṇa;
After the nirvana of that Buddha, Lord of the World,
The monk always kept this meditation.

Then I was a king, of princely stock;
In a dream I heard of this meditation:
"The monk Varuṇa has this sutra;
You, O King, should accept this mental concentration
from him."

When I awoke from the dream I went in search of him,
And straightaway met the monk who held the meditation.
Then I removed my hair and beard, became an ascetic,
And studied for eight thousand years so as to hear it once.

For years whose number reached a full eighty thousand,
I made offerings to and served this monk;
At the time, conditions due to Māra frequently arose,
And from the first I never once heard it.

Therefore, monks and nuns,
Men of pure faith and women of pure faith,
I commit this sutra-dharma to you.
When you hear this meditation, quickly take it up!

Always honor the teacher who practises and keeps this Dharma
Unremittingly for a whole aeon;
For the sake of the Way, do not regard a thousand million years as a hardship;
You shall succeed in hearing this Dharma, this meditation.

Robes and beds by the millions,
And food which the monk begs from house to house—
Make offerings of them to the teacher of Dharma;
If you are energetic in this way you will master the meditation.

Whatever lamps, food, and drink you obtain,
Gold, silver, and precious gems, offer them all.
If you should cut off your own flesh
To make an offering of it, how much more so food and drink?

When the intelligent person obtains the Dharma he quickly takes it up,
He accepts and studies the sutra volumes repeatedly.
This meditation is difficult to find;
For millions and billions of aeons you should constantly seek it.

Wherever you circulate, listen to this Dharma;
You should disclose it widely to students;

Even if for a thousand million billion aeons
One looks for this meditation, it is difficult to hear.

If worlds as numerous as the sands of the Ganges
Were filled with precious gems and used as a gift,
And if someone accepted one verse of this and preached it,
The merit of that reverent recitation would exceed the
former.

Chapter XVI

The Seal of the Buddha

Thereupon the Buddha said to Bhadrapāla: "Any bodhisattvas who hear this meditation, should, when they hear it, rejoice over it, and they should study it. Having studied it, they should, by means of the Buddha's numinous power, cause others to study it. They should make a fine copy of this meditation on plain silk, they should get the seal of the Buddha and seal it, and they should make offerings to it properly. 919b6

"What is the seal of the Buddha? It is, namely, that which cannot act, is without cravings, without desires, without conceptual thoughts, without attachments, without aspirations, without rebirth, without preferences, birthless, nonexistent, non-grasping, non-caring, unabiding, unobstructed, nonexistent, unbound, exhausted of what exists, exhausted of desires, not produced from anywhere, imperishable, indestructible, ineradicable, the essence of the Way, and the root of the Way. As to this seal, the arhats and the pratyekabuddhas cannot destroy it, cannot ruin it, and cannot impair it. Fools then doubt this seal. This seal is the seal of the Buddha."

The Buddha said: "Just now, as I have been preaching this meditation, eighteen hundred million gods, Asura spirits, dragons, and human beings have all attained the Way of the stream-enterer, eight hundred monks have all attained the Way of the arhat, five hundred nuns have all attained the Way of the arhat, ten thousand bodhisattvas have all mastered this meditation, and have all attained happiness in dharmas which are not produced from anywhere and have established themselves in it; and twelve thousand bodhisattvas will never regress."

The Buddha spoke to Śāriputra, Mahāmaudgalyāyana, the monk Ānanda, the bodhisattva Bhadrapāla, the bodhisattva Ratnākara, the bodhisattva Guhagupta, the bodhisattva Naradatta, the bodhisattva SusΔma, the bodhisattva Mahāsusārthavāha, the bodhisattva Indradatta, and the bodhisattva Varu√adeva. The Buddha said: "I, who have for innumerable aeons been seeking the Way of the Buddha, and who have now attained Buddhahood, commit this sutra to you. Study it, recite it, preserve it, cultivate it, and do not forget it. Bhadrapāla, any bodhisattvas who study this meditation should study it all calmly and carefully. If they wish to hear it, they should hear it all. If they preach it to other people, they should preach 919c
it all."

When the Buddha had preached the sutra, the bodhisattva Bhadrapāla and the others, Śāriputra, Mahāmaudgalyāyana, the monk Ānanda and the others, as well as the gods, Asuras, dragons, spirits, and human beings all rejoiced greatly, came forward to make obeisance to the Buddha, and departed.

Here Ends Fascicle Three
of The Pratyutpanna Samādhi Sutra

Glossary

Akaniṣṭha: The fourth and highest heaven in the Realm of Form.

arhat: A person who has attained nirvana. Arhatship is the highest spiritual achievement according to mainstream Buddhism.

Asura: A class of demonic beings who are in constant conflict with the gods. One of the six destinies of beings, and often translated as "titan" or "demi-god."

Bhadrakalpa: The Auspicious Aeon, the name of the present age.

bodhisattva: A person who aspires to become a Buddha.

brahman: A member of the priestly class in Indian society.

Buddha-field: The world in which a Buddha lives and teaches.

devaputra: The son of a god, a heavenly being.

Dharma: (1) The law which enables all existence and creation; (2) the Truth; (3) the essential quality or nature of all phenomena.

dharmas: (1) The principles, factors of existence, or realities in terms of which human experience can be analysed; (2) the teachings (of a Buddha), which taken together constitute the Dharma; or (3) the qualities or attainments (of a Buddha).

dragon (*nāga*): A type of serpent deity often believed to live in bodies of water.

eight advantages: Possibly the eight spheres of sovereignty, eight ways in which one masters one's perceptions of external forms.

eightfold fast: A special observance for lay practitioners, often involving temporary residence at a monastery and the assumption of extra precepts (bringing the total to eight).

eight forms of energy: The opposite of the eight forms of sloth (q.v.).

eight forms of sloth: Eight occasions when one might not exert oneself, i.e., when one does not wish to tire oneself by engaging in, or feels already tired from having engaged in, physical work (1-2) or travel (3-4), when one is tired after not getting enough food (5), after getting enough (6), from being slightly ill (7), or after recovering from an illness (8).

eight places of hardship: Eight situations in which one cannot achieve salvation, i.e., when one is born as an animal, a departed spirit, a hell-dweller, or a god; when one is born in an uncivilized border region, with defective faculties, with a perversely heretical outlook, or at a time when there is no Buddha.

eight thoughts of the man of the Way: The reflection that the Dharma is for the person who has few desires, knows contentment, is secluded from society, is energetic, mindful, composed, wise, and mentally focused.

five aggregates (*skandhas*): Five components of the human psycho-physical personality, viz. form (or matter), feelings, conceptions (or thoughts), karmic formations (Lokakṣema: birth-and-death), and consciousness.

five desires: Desire for the objects of the five senses.

five destinies: The five realms in which one may be reborn are those of the gods, humans, animals, departed spirits, and hell-dwellers (the last three are regarded as evil destinies). Sometimes the Asuras are added as a sixth destiny.

five obscurations: Five hindrances or obstacles to spiritual development, being sensual desire, malice, slothfulness, mental agitation, and doubt.

five practices: Possibly the five spheres of emancipation, according to which a person achieves liberation while being taught the Dharma, while teaching it to others, while repeating it alone, while reflecting on it, or while meditating on some other meditation device.

five precepts: Not to take life, steal, engage in sexual misconduct, tell lies, or consume intoxicants.

four classes: Monks, nuns, laymen, and laywomen.

four elements: Earth, water, fire, wind. Sometimes space is added as a fifth.

four great ones. *See* four elements.

four stoppings of thought: Four foundations or applications of mindfulness.

Gandharva: A class of mythical beings, celestial musicians.

Garuḍa: A class of mythical beings, half human and half bird.

happiness in dharmas which do not come into existence or are not produced (*anutpattika-dharma-kṣānti*): Also translated as patient acceptance of these dharmas or of non-origination, this is a decisive realisation by the bodhisattva of the emptiness of all dharmas, i.e., the absence of inherent existence in them.

infinites (*apramāṇa* or *brahma-vihāra*): The meditative cultivation of four attitudes, i.e. limitless friendliness or love, compassion, sympathetic joy, and equanimity (Lokakṣema: circumspection).

Jambudvīpa: The southern continent of the Buddhist cosmos.

Kinnara: A class of mythical beings, either half human and half bird or half human and half horse, who make celestial music.

kṣatriya: A member of the warrior or ruler class in Indian society.

Kumbhāṇḍa: A class of malevolent mythical beings.

Mahayana: Great Way or Great Vehicle, denoting that form of Buddhism which emphasises the bodhisattva path to full Buddhahood. This is contrasted with the supposedly inferior way of the arhats and the pratyekabuddhas (q.v.).

Mahoraga: A class of snake-like mythical beings.

Maitreya: The next Buddha to appear in this world.

Māra: The Buddhist equivalent of the Devil, the personification of death and desire; in the plural this term refers to a class of such beings.

Meru: The gigantic mountain that rises in the center of the Buddhist cosmos.

nine reflections: Possibly the ninefold meditation on the repulsive, which contemplates various stages in the decomposition of a corpse.

nine vexations: Nine occasions for ill-will, i.e., the thought that another person has done, is doing, or will do either harm to oneself (1-3), or harm to a loved one (4-6), or good to an enemy (7-9).

nonaction: A Taoist term used for liberation or nirvana.

non-regression: A stage in the career of a bodhisattva after reaching which there can be no turning back from the achievement of Buddhahood.

original nonbeing (*tathatā*): Reality or actuality, expressed by the Chinese notion of primal undifferentiated being.

Parinirvāṇa: The death or passing into final liberation (of the Buddha).

pratyekabuddha: A person who attains awakening by his or her own efforts, but does not subsequently teach others so as to bring them to liberation.

samādhi: A state of meditative concentration.

six tastes: In this context the six ways of being considerate or sociable, i.e., being friendly to one's fellow practitioners in thought, word, and deed, sharing one's goods with them, living virtuously, and holding to the truth.

six transcendences (*pāramitā*): Six perfections, being those of giving or liberality, morality (or keeping the precepts), patient acceptance or forbearance, energy or vigor, meditation (Lokakṣema: single-mindedness), and wisdom.

stream-enterer: A person who has achieved a preliminary realization of the truth such that he or she will be reborn seven more times at most.

stupa: A reliquary, a roughly hemispherical structure enshrining the relics of the Buddha or other figures, or copies of the Buddhist scriptures.

Sumeru. *See* Meru.

sutra-dharmas: A composite term often used by Lokakṣema to translate the Sanskrit term dharma, indicating dharmas both as teachings or scriptures and as truths or principles of existence.

sutras: Canonical discourses or scriptures delivered by the Buddha.

Tathāgata: Realized One, a title of the Buddha.

ten evils: Ten unwholesome actions, i.e., taking life, theft, sexual misconduct, lying, slander, harsh speech, frivolous talk, avarice, malice, wrong views.

ten goods: Ten meritorious actions, i.e., abstaining from the ten evils (q.v.).

ten powers: Ten special abilities possessed by a Buddha.

ten quarters: The four points of the compass, the four intermediate points, the zenith, and the nadir.

thirty-two marks: Special physical characteristics found on the body of a Buddha or a Universal Monarch, each one supposedly produced by a hundred meritorious acts.

Three Ages: The past, the present, and the future.

Three Realms: The rebirth cosmos, which is divided into the Realm of Desire, the Realm of Form, and the Realm of the Formless.

Three Spheres. *See* Three Realms.

Three Thousand Great Thousand Realms: A vast assembly of world-systems, resembling a galaxy.

three thousand lands: A shorthand term for a vast assembly of world-systems.

Triple World. *See* Three Realms.

twelve diminishers. *See* twelve sense-fields.

twelve sense-fields or "entrances": The six senses (including the mind as the sixth) and their respective objects (with dharmas being the object of mind).

Way: Chinese term used for awakening or enlightenment (*bodhi*). Sometimes referred to as the Great Way (which may also denote the Mahayana, q.v.).

wearers of white: The laity, people not ordained into the Buddhist order or following any other ascetic paths.

Yakṣa: A class of mythical beings. Sometimes thought to be a type of tree-spirit.

Endnotes

1. On the assumption that large combination numbers of this type are not intended to be mathematically precise, the following formal equivalents are used in this translation to avoid excessive clumsiness: 'myriad' for Chinese *wan* (ten thousand), 'million' for Chinese *yi* (either one hundred thousand or one hundred million) or Sanskrit *koṭi* (strictly, ten million), and 'billion' for Sanskrit *nayuta* (usually one hundred thousand million). (p. 8)

2. An alternative translation is 'not wishing to hear that by means of which animals come to be born.' This is possibly Lokakṣema's gloss on what is known in Pali as *tiracchāna-kathā* or 'animal talk', i.e., low or vulgar conversation or gossip about worldly matters. (p. 16)

3. An alternative translation is '(Regarding) all the Buddhas as one; in one's thinking (or mindfulness) entering a state of freedom from obstruction.' All versions are rather obscure at this point. (p. 17)

4. To clarify the meaning of the text at this point, one could say that the Buddha preaches the Dharma of the indestructability or imperishability of form (or matter), the other four *skandha*s or constituents of existence, and so on. These components of our experience are indestructible insofar as they are unproduced in the first place, being empty of essence. The notion of imperishability appears to have been quite an important theme in a number of Mahayana sutras. (p.19)

5. The Chinese word *changji* means literally 'singing girl' or 'prostitute', but this can hardly have been the original sense. One must assume that singing or vocal music is what Lokakṣema had in mind here. (p. 24)

6. The text is obscure. An alternative rendering—seeing a possible echo from the *Dao de jing*—is 'Do not seek anything in your practice, and there will be nothing that is not sought.' (p. 38)

7. Throughout this chapter and elsewhere in this and other translations, Lokakṣema uses both *huanxi* ('to rejoice') or *zhu(qi)-huanxi* ('to help (one) to rejoice') and *quanzhu* ('to encourage') to convey the various nuances of the concept of *anumodanā*, the act of sympathetic rejoicing, thanksgiving or applause which is instrumental in ritual operations designed to transfer or redirect merit. (p. 89)

Bibliography

Harrison, Paul. *The Tibetan Text of the Pratyutpanna-Buddha-Saṃmukhāvasthita-Samādhi-Sūtra.* Studia Philologica Buddhica, Monograph Series, I. Tokyo: The Reiyūkai Library, 1978.

———. "*Buddhānusmṛti* in the *Pratyutpanna-buddha-saṃmukhāvasthita-samādhi-sūtra.*" *Journal of Indian Philosophy* 6 (1978): 35-57.

———. *The Samādhi of Direct Encounter with the Buddhas of the Present: An Annotated English Translation of the Tibetan Version of the* Pratyutpanna-Buddha-Saṃmukhāvasthita-Samādhi-Sūtra *with Several Appendices Relating to the History of the Text.* Studia Philologica Buddhica, Monograph Series, V. Tokyo: The International Institute for Buddhist Studies, 1990.

———. "Commemoration and Identification in *Buddhānusmṛti.*" In *In the Mirror of Memory: Reflections on Mindfulness and Remembrance in Indian and Tibetan Buddhism.* Edited by Janet Gyatso. New York: SUNY Press, 1992.

———. "The Earliest Chinese Translations of Mahāyāna Sūtras: Some Notes on the Works of Lokakṣema." *Buddhist Studies Review* 10 (2) (1993): 135-177.

Kajiyama, Yūichi. "Hanju-zanmai-kyō: amidabutsu-shinkō to kū no shisō (The *Pratyutpanna-samādhi-sūtra*: Faith in the Buddha Amitābha and the philosophy of emptiness)". In *Jōdo-bukkyō no shisō (Pure Land Buddhist Thought).* Translated by Sueki Fumihiko and Kajiyama Yūichi. Vol. 2 . Tokyo: Kodansha, 1992. An extensive study of the text with a partial translation of the Tibetan version (in Japanese).

Index

BDK English Tripiṭaka 25-III

The Śūraṅgama Samādhi Sutra

Translated by

Kumārajīva

Translated from the Chinese

(Taishō Volume 15, Number 642)

by

John McRae

**Numata Center
for Buddhist Translation and Research
1998**

Contents

Translator's Introduction

The Śūraṅgama Samādhi Sūtra is an exquisite religious scripture. One of the most profound of all Mahāyāna texts, it depicts a vision of Buddhism that is thoroughly transcendent and at the same time uniquely humanistic. Here the Buddha Śākyamuni is no mere historical personage, but the one eternal cosmic Buddha who is the source of all other Buddhas. The Dharma Śākyamuni teaches is the Śūraṅgama Samādhi, the meditative concentration of the "heroic march" to Buddhahood, which is presented in overwhelmingly lavish terms as the very key to the enlightenment of the Buddhas and all of their awesome spiritual power. And the prize that awaits those who practice and achieve mastery of this incredible samādhi is not merely enlightenment in individual terms, but the insurpassable and perfect enlightenment of Buddhahood itself. Indeed, this text implies it would be impossible to remain in any Hīnayānist state of enlightened extinction, since the Śūraṅgama Samādhi even gives the Buddha the power to recall the Pratyekabuddhas (those who are enlightened by their own efforts and who pass into extinction without teaching others), and Arhats (those who complete the entire Hīnayāna path to achieve total Nirvāṇic extinction) from their religious comas to achieve perfect Buddhahood.

The text is classically Mahāyāna in format and structure. It begins with a grand assembly on Mount Gṛdhrakūṭa (Vulture Peak), where the Buddha is surrounded by great numbers of bhikṣus, Bodhisattvas, and other beings. The dialogue begins with a question by a Bodhisattva named Resolute Mind (one of several figures who appear here who are not known in other texts), then proceeds involving a number of participants, including Bodhisattvas, Śrāvakas (the human disciples of the Buddha identified with the Hīnayāna), gods, and goddesses. It also uses several different supernatural manifestations, such as the simultaneous offering of innumerable elaborate chairs for the Buddha by all the most highly ranked gods present, the appearance of Māra bound hand and foot and unable at first to attend the preaching of the Sūtra, and the manifestation of the palaces of Māra and innumerable Indra gods. The grand climax of all these is the Buddha's manifestation of all the innumerable Buddhas of the ten directions, shining with light and surrounded by their assemblies, who then offer flowers to form canopies over the heads of these Buddhas, first over Śākyamuni and then over all the others. This magnificent epiphany is presented as part of a dramatic hesitation toward the end of the dialogue, when some of the Bodhisattvas in Śākyamuni's assembly become discouraged by the apparent difficulty of the path to Buddhahood being described. Finally, there is the charge to Ānanda to preach the Sūtra, which is also carried up by one of the many Indra kings who appear in the text. The incomparable merits of copying, reciting, and teaching the Sūtra are extolled, and as the scene closes countless numbers of sentient beings generate the Bodhicitta, the intention to achieve insurpassable and perfect enlightenment, eighteen thousand Bodhisattvas attain the Śūraṅgama Samādhi, an equal number of bhikṣus and bhikṣunis (monks and nuns) attain Arhatship, and even greater numbers of laypeople and gods attain different levels of understanding.

From the very beginning of the dialogue it is apparent that this Sūtra (or, rather, its anonymous author) grapples with a fundamental problem that faced the practitioners of the Mahāyāna: how to account for the apparently dismal spiritual fates of Hīnayānist practitioners, the Śrāvakas, Pratyekabuddhas, and Arhats. Resolute Mind Bodhisattva's opening question concerns whether or not there exists a samādhi that causes Bodhisattvas to rapidly achieve perfect enlightenment, while at the same time allowing beings of lesser aspirations to practice successfully according to their own understanding even as they proceed along the Mahāyāna path. We learn that this is indeed one of the cardinal attributes of the Śūraṅgama Samādhi, so that those who appear to practice and even believe themselves to be practicing the so-called Hīnayāna will actually achieve Buddhahood according to the Mahāyāna at some point in the future. Even more, as the text proceeds we learn that the Śūraṅgama Samādhi allows many enlightened beings to manifest themselves in any number of worldly shapes for the purpose of teaching sentient beings, so that gods, kings, monks, and laypeople may actually be forms taken by the enlightened for salvific purposes. The ultimate variation on this theme is the information given toward the end of the scripture that Mañjuśrī Bodhisattva was actually a perfectly enlightened Buddha (his name and the particulars of his true identity are given) who had manifested himself as a Pratyekabuddha in thirty-six billion different lifetimes in order to teach sentient beings.

This is a magnificent contradiction of the Buddhist doctrinal convention—explicitly refuted in the text—that entry into Nirvāṇa as a Pratyekabuddha or Arhat represents a spiritual dead end, a total extinction from which one cannot return. (The discouragement felt by some of the Buddha's listeners at the end of the text, already mentioned above, is actually that they might have to labor mightily for the achievement of the Śūraṅgama Samādhi yet still get sidetracked into a lesser enlightenment.) This text simply cannot allow the Hīnayānist to remain in such a spiritual void, and it does not stop with merely saying that they are to be retrieved from their extinctions, but goes on to describe a religious world in which personal identity may be adopted and manifested at will for teaching purposes. Given such thoroughgoing fluidity of identity, the earlier doctrinal conventions about the distinctiveness and irreversibility of different spiritual paths are not just rejected but thoroughly transformed.

There are several other themes present in this Sūtra that should not go unmentioned. The existence of innumerable other Buddha lands is basic to the philosophy of the scripture, since Bodhisattvas have to worship other Buddhas in order to achieve their own Buddhahood. Several other Buddha lands are mentioned by name and described, although the only one known widely from other sources is the Wondrous Joy world of the Buddha Akṣobhya. It is especially interesting to notice, then, that Amitābha/Amitāyus and his Sukhāvatī are unmentioned. Also, great significance is placed on the Buddha's bestowal of the prediction of future Buddhahood throughout the text, and even Māra is the recipient of such a prediction—before he has even sincerely generated the Bodhicitta. Offerings are extremely important in this text, and they seem to receive greater weight than other forms of religious praxis. The spiritual identity and fate of women is touched on in a couple of the scripture's anecdotes, most particularly regarding two hundred goddesses introduced as attendants to Māra, who are revealed by the Buddha to have already "planted good roots" under five hundred Buddhas in the past. The Buddha goes on to predict that they will make offerings to innumerable Buddhas in the future and after seven hundred eons will themselves achieve Buddhahood. Although the Buddha states that their next lifetimes will be as human females serving the future Buddha Maitreya, their transformation into male form is never explicitly mentioned.

But all these features are of secondary importance to the religious significance of the Śūraṅgama Samādhi itself. What are we to make of this incredible and spectacular concentration? Indeed, the explanation of the Śūraṅgama Samādhi is so conceptually abstruse that it amounts to an encapsulation of the entirety of the Mahāyāna Buddhist path. The description of how one learns it begins with a common simile for meditation practice, the progressive training in archery so that one can hit even small targets. Following this, the practitioner is told to study a sequence that proceeds rapidly through the mind of ecstasy, the profound mind, great sympathy, great compassion, and so forth, through the five supernatural "penetrations" and the six Mahāyāna Perfections, so that he achieves forbearance of the birthlessness of the dharmas and thus receives a prediction of Buddhahood. At this point, the practitioner is at the eighth Bodhisattva stage, but it is only at the tenth stage that he is able to attain the Śūraṅgama Samādhi. This is compared to perfect mastery of archery, in which one can consistently hit targets smaller than a single hair. No doubt some of the Buddha's listeners became discouraged!

Presumably, one way to approach this mind-boggling complexity is to consider it a vehicle for the transmission of ideas about emptiness [śūnyatā] and the subtle profundity of the Bodhisattva ideal. Here I can do no better than to let the reader experience the text directly, to imbibe of its inestimable spiritual power.

Fascicle I

Translated by the Kuchean Tripiṭaka Master Kumārajīva during the Later Ch'in [Dynasty]

Thus have I heard. At one time the Buddha was on Mount Gṛdhrakūṭa near Rājagṛha, with thirty-two thousand great *bhikṣus* in attendance. There were also seventy-two thousand Bodhisattva Mahāsattvas there who were known to the assembly and who had mastered *dhāraṇī,* were accomplished in the discrimination [of spiritual matters], and took unlimited pleasure in preaching [the Dharma]. They resided in samādhi without any vacillation, well comprehended the inexhaustible wisdoms, had achieved profound forbearance of [the inherent birthlessness of] all dharmas, had attained profound insight into the Dharma, and had completed all the training that there is to be undertaken in all the excellent Dharmas during all the limitless and innumerable eons. They had subjugated the hordes of demons [Māras] and had vanquished their enemies. They had incorporated within themselves that which is most honored and had ornamented and purified the Buddha lands. They possessed great compassion, had ornamented their bodies with the various marks [of enlightened beings], and had with great endeavor attained the other shore [of Nirvāṇa]. Well did they know all the verbal expedient means [of teaching], and their practice of the ceremonial deportments was complete and pure. They all had achieved residence in the three emancipations and had penetrated the three periods of time with their unhindered wisdom. They had generated the determination not to abandon all [sentient beings], remembered the purport of the doctrines, and possessed the tolerant forbearance of wisdom. Such was the virtue of all these Bodhisattvas. 629b14

Their names were Turns the Wheel of the Dharma without Regressing Bodhisattva, Generating the Intention [to Achieve Enlightenment] That Constitutes Turning the Wheel of the Dharma Bodhisattva, Turns the Wheel of the Dharma without Hindrance Bodhisattva, Purity That Transcends Defilement Bodhisattva, Obstructions Eradicated Bodhisattva, Manifests Pure Deportment and Perceives All with Loving Joy Bodhisattva, Mind of a Wondrous and Dignified King Bodhisattva, Does Not Delude All Sentient Beings Bodhisattva, Mind Like an Ocean of Unlimited Merit Bodhisattva, Senses Always Composed and Not Disordered Bodhisattva, True Sound Bodhisattva, Praised by All the Gods Bodhi-
629c sattva, Autonomous King of *Dhāraṇī* Bodhisattva, Ornamented with Discernment Bodhisattva, the Dharma Prince Mañjuśrī Bodhisattva, Maitreya Bodhisattva, King of Mount Sumeru Bodhisattva, Pure Mind of the Ocean of Virtues and Treasured Dignity Bodhisattva, Greatly Dignified and Pure Bodhisattva, Great Characteristic Bodhisattva, Characteristic of Refulgence Bodhisattva, Pure Mind Bodhisattva, Joyous King Bodhisattva, Resolute Energy Bodhisattva, and Resolute Mind Bodhisattva.

There were seventy-two thousand such Bodhisattva Mahāsattvas, plus all the Indra gods, Brahmā gods, and world-protecting heavenly kings of the great trichiliocosm, as well as gods, dragons, *yakṣa*s, *gandharva*s, *asura*s, *garuḍa*s, *kiṃnara*s, and *mahoraga*s, both human and nonhuman beings. All those who were recognized by the congregation, who had planted many types of good roots, and who took joy in the Mahāyāna had come to the assembly.

At that time, while in the great assembly, Resolute Mind Bodhisattva had the following thought: "I should now ask the Tathāgata [about the Dharma]. By such inquiries will I protect the seed of the Buddha, the seed of the Dharma, and the seed of the Saṅgha. By rendering the palaces of the demons invisible and subjugating [all] those with great arrogance, those who have not yet planted the good roots [for spiritual growth] will be made to do so now. Those who have planted good roots will have them made to grow. Anyone who has not yet generated the intention to achieve unsurpassable and perfect enlightenment [on behalf of all sentient beings] (Bodhicitta) will be induced to do so now. Those who have already generated this intention should not be allowed to regress. Those who have not regressed should be made to attain rapidly the unsurpassable and perfect enlightenment. Those who presume to possess some [degree of] attainment and who are mired [*lit.*, reside] in ascriptive views should all generate an attitude of detachment [from such views]. Those who take pleasure in the lesser Dharma (the Hīnayāna) should be made not to doubt the great Dharma (the Mahāyāna.) Those who take pleasure in the great Dharma should be inspired to generate joy."

After thinking thus, [Resolute Mind Bodhisattva] arose from his seat, arranged his robe over his right shoulder, and touched his right knee to the ground. Holding his palms together [in the *añjali-mudrā*] he addressed the Buddha as follows: "O World-Honored One, I would like to ask a few questions regarding the Tathāgata's teaching. I beseech you to hear my inquiries." The Buddha told Resolute Mind: "I will answer your questions in a way that will give you joy [in the Dharma]."

Resolute Mind Bodhisattva then said to the Buddha: "O World-Honored One, is there a samādhi that can cause Bodhisattvas to achieve unsurpassable and perfect enlightenment rapidly; that allows one always to see the Buddhas face to face; that allows one to illuminate all the ten directions with [great] brilliance; that gives one an autonomous mastery of wisdom [*hui*] by which the demons may be destroyed; and that allows one to achieve an autonomous mastery of wisdom [*chih*], to attain spontaneous wisdom [*tzu-jan chih*], and to attain birthless wisdom, which cannot be attained from any other source? Its uninterruptible [power of] discernment should allow one to achieve the bases of supernormal power and limitless rebirths. Those who would take pleasure in being Śrāvakas (Hīnayānists) will be shown the Vehicle of the Śrāvaka; those who would take pleasure in being Pratyekabuddhas will be shown the Vehicle of the Pratyekabuddha; and those who would take pleasure in the Great Vehicle will be shown the Mahāyāna.

They will penetrate the Dharma of the Śrāvaka but will not enter the path of the Śrāvaka; they will penetrate the Dharma of the Pratyekabuddha but will not enter the path of the Pratyekabuddha;
630a they will penetrate the Dharma of the Buddhas but will not proceed to ultimate and final extinction. While manifesting the form and deportment of Śrāvakas, within themselves they will not depart from their intention to achieve Buddhahood; while manifesting the form and deportment of Pratyekabuddhas, within themselves they will not depart from the Great Compassion of the Buddhas. Using the phantasmagorical power of samādhi, they will manifest the form and deportment of Tathāgatas. Using the power of their good roots, they will manifest themselves residing in the Tuṣita heaven, receiving their final bodies, entering into wombs, being born, leaving home, and sitting in the places of enlightenment [*bodhimaṇḍa*] of Buddhas. Using the power of their profound wisdom, they will manifest the turning of the Wheel of the Dharma; with the power of their expedient means, they will manifest the entry into Nirvāṇa; with the power of samādhi, they will manifest the distribution of relics [*śarīra*]; and with the power of their original vows, they will manifest the final extinction of [all the multifarious] dharmas [of their personal existence]. Although it shall be so, O World-Honored One, what samādhi should Bodhisattvas practice in order to manifest these meritorious affairs without actually entering into ultimate Nirvāṇa?"

The Buddha told Resolute Mind Bodhisattva: "Excellent, excellent! O Resolute Mind, that you can ask the Tathāgata such a question indicates that you can greatly benefit and comfort sentient beings, that you have pity on the world, and that you will aid gods and humans. A Bodhisattva is to be of benefit [to others] in both present and future. You should realize that to have such profound good roots you must have made offerings to and associated intimately with limitless hundreds and thousands and hundred-millions of Buddhas in the past. You have practiced all the paths and subjugated the enemies; you have attained autonomous mastery of wisdom in the Dharma of the Buddhas; you have taught and protected the assemblies of Bodhisattvas; and you already know the Dharma Treasury of All the Buddhas. In the past you have engaged in dialogue before Buddhas as limitless as the number of grains of sand in the River Ganges. O Resolute Mind, in the present assembly I see no dragon, *yakṣa, gandharva,* Śrāvaka, or Pratyekabuddha able to ask such a question. Only those of great adornment [of the path] such as yourself are able to formulate questions such as this. You should now listen clearly and think well on this, for I will now explain for you how the Bodhisattvas accomplish their samādhi so as to achieve merits even greater than those you describe."

Resolute Mind said to the Buddha: "I beseech you to let us hear [this teaching]."

The Buddha said to Resolute Mind: "There is a samādhi by the name of Śūraṅgama (heroic march). All Bodhisattvas who achieve this samādhi will, as you have described, be able to manifest Parinirvāṇa without undergoing eternal extinction. They will be able to manifest the various forms without destroying the characteristics of form. They will be able to wander throughout all the Buddha lands without any discrimination with regard to those lands. They will all be able to meet all the Buddhas but without discrimination with regard to the universally equivalent [*p'ing-teng, samatā*] essence of the Dharma [*fa-hsing, dharmatā*]. They will manifest universal accomplishment of all the practices but will well realize the purity of those practices. They will be the very highest of those most honored by the gods and humans but will be without any self-conceit, pride, or laxity. They will manifest autonomous mastery of all the demonic powers but will not depend on demonic practices. They will practice throughout all the triple realm (the desire, form, and formless realms) but will lack any vacillation with regard to the characteristics of the dharmas. They will manifest rebirth in all the various modes of 630b
existence but will not discriminate with regard to the characteristics of those modes. They will be skilled in the explanation of all the phrases of the Dharma and able to reveal their meanings in

words, but they will realize that words have [*lit.*, enter into] the characteristic of universal equivalence and have no discrimination with regard to words. They will always remain in meditation as they manifest their teachings to sentient beings. They will practice total forbearance of the birthlessness of all dharmas but preach that all dharmas have the characteristics of generation and extinction. They will walk alone, without fear, like lions."

At that time all the Indra gods, Brahmā gods, and world-protecting heavenly kings and everyone else in the great assembly had the following thought: "We have never before heard even the name of this samādhi; how could we have ever heard an explanation of its meaning? Now we can see the Buddha and will joyfully receive good [spiritual] benefit through hearing him preach the name of the Śūraṅgama Samādhi. If a good man or woman seeking the enlightenment of Buddhahood were to hear the doctrine of the Śūraṅgama Samādhi and to understand and accept it without doubt, then he or she would certainly never regress on the path to enlightenment. How much more so for those who accept it, maintain it, and recite it, and who teach it to others and practice it as it has been taught!"

At that time the Indra gods, Brahmā gods, and world-protecting heavenly kings all had the following thought: "I will now prepare for the Buddha a Lion's Seat, a seat of the True Dharma, a seat for the most exalted of persons, a great ornamented seat, a great seat for the turning of the Wheel of the Dharma, so that the Tathāgata can preach the Śūraṅgama Samādhi on this seat prepared by me." Every one of them had the same thought, each thinking that he was the only one able to prepare the Lion's Seat for the Tathāgata and that the others were unable to do so. At that time the Indra gods, Brahmā gods, and world-protecting heavenly kings each prepared a Lion's Seat for the Tathāgata, ornamenting it in purity and making it correct and high, draping the top with robes made with immeasurable treasures, each one of them covering the seat with canopies made with many wondrous treasures. There were also handrails made with various precious things. To the right and left of each seat were matching rows of innumerable precious trees, with their leaves and branches intertwined. From them hung canopies, which spread out together into a great cover made of treasures. From ropes made of various treasures hung many precious bells. Many types of wondrous flowers were scattered about the top of the seat, and a mixture of incenses from the heavens was burning, adding its fragrance. A profusion of light gleamed from the gold, silver, and many precious things, and none of the many types of pure and beautiful things were omitted. In the space of an instant there appeared before the Tathāgata eighty-four thousand billion *nayuta*s of such precious Lion's Seats, and none of them interfered with any of the other seats in the assembly. Each individual god was unable to see the other seats, and each thought as follows: "I alone have prepared the Lion's Seat for the Buddha. The Buddha will now preach the Śūraṅgama Samādhi on the seat I have prepared for him."

At that time the Indra gods, Brahmā gods, and world-protecting heavenly kings, having finished preparing the seats, each addressed the Buddha as follows: "I beg the Tathāgata to sit upon the seat I have prepared and preach the Śūraṅgama Samādhi." The World-Honored One then manifested his great supernormal power and sat upon all the eighty-four thousand billion *nayuta*s of Lion's Seats, so that each and every god saw the Buddha sitting 630c
on the seat he had prepared, but did not see the other seats. One of the Indra gods said to the others: "See the Tathāgata sitting upon the seat I have prepared." Then all the Indra gods, Brahmā gods, and world-protecting heavenly kings said to each other: "See the Tathāgata sitting upon the seat I have prepared." One Indra said: "The Tathāgata is now sitting on the seat I have prepared, not on yours."

At that time the Tathāgata, wishing to help the many Indra gods, Brahmā gods, and world-protecting heavenly kings overcome their karmic bonds from the past [*lit.*, to save them from past conditions], wanting to manifest a small part of the power of the Śūraṅgama Samādhi, and in order to generate the practice of the

Mahāyāna, made everyone in the assembly see that the Tathāgata was sitting on all the other eighty-four thousand billion *nayuta*s of precious Lion's Seats. Everyone in the assembly experienced great joy such as they had never felt before, and they all arose from their seats, put their hands together, and worshipped the Buddha, saying: "Excellent, O World-Honored One! Your supernormal abilities are immeasurable! You have allowed the many gods to fulfill their desires!" Seeing the Buddha's divine power, the gods who had prepared seats for the Tathāgata all generated the aspiration to achieve unsurpassable and perfect enlightenment on behalf of all sentient beings. In unison, they said to the Buddha: "O World-Honored One, we have now generated the intention to achieve unsurpassable and perfect enlightenment on behalf of all sentient beings in order to make an offering to the Tathāgata, to eradicate all the afflictions of sentient beings, to protect the True Dharma, and to prevent the Buddha's seed from being eradicated. We wish to be able to exercise such supernormal powers of a Buddha in the future, to be able to perform transformations such as the Tathāgata has done now." The Buddha then praised those gods, saying: "Excellent, excellent! As you have said, out of the wish to benefit all sentient beings, you have now generated the aspiration to achieve unsurpassable and perfect enlightenment. This is the highest offering that can be made to the Tathāgata."

At that time there was a Brahmā king within the assembly named Equivalent Practice, who addressed the Buddha, saying, "O World-Honored One, which Tathāgata is the real one, the one on the seat I have prepared, or one on another seat?" The Buddha told Equivalent Practice, "All the dharmas are empty, like phantasms, and only exist in conjunction with each other. They have no creator, but arise entirely due to the discrimination of conceptual thought. Because there is no master [of consciousness, the myriad dharmas] appear according to one's thoughts. All the Tathāgatas are real.

"What is real? All these Tathāgatas are fundamentally not born, and so they are real. All these Tathāgatas will not cease to exist in the future, and so they are real. These Tathāgatas are not collocations of the four elements, and so they are real. Nor are they collocations of the *skandhas*, *āyatanas*, and *dhātus*, and so they are real. There are no differentiations of first, middle, and last between these Tathāgatas, and so they are real.

"O Brahmā king, these Tathāgatas are without differentiation. Why? The form [*skandhas*] of these Tathāgatas are suchlike, and hence they are equivalent. The feelings, perceptions, impulses, and consciousness [*skandhas*] of these Tathāgatas are suchlike, and hence they are equivalent. Because of these reasons, they are equivalent. The pasts of these Tathāgatas are suchlike, and hence they 631a
are equivalent. Their futures are suchlike, and hence they are equivalent. Their presents are suchlike, and hence they are equivalent. Being like phantasmagorical dharmas, they are equivalent. Being like shadow dharmas, they are equivalent. Being dharmas that cannot exist, they are equivalent. With nowhere that they came from and nowhere that they go to, they are equivalent. For these reasons, these Tathāgatas are called equivalent. Just as all dharmas are equivalent, so are all these Tathāgatas. Just as all sentient beings are equivalent, so are all these Tathāgatas. Just as the Buddhas of all the worlds are equivalent, so are all these Tathāgatas. Just as all the worlds are equivalent, so are all these Tathāgatas. For these reasons, the Buddhas are called equivalent. O Brahmā king, these Tathāgatas are nothing more than the Suchness of all the dharmas, and so they are called equivalent. You should realize, Brahmā king, that the Tathāgata knows all the myriad dharmas to be equivalent, and for this reason the Tathāgata is called equivalent with regard to all the myriad dharmas."

Equivalent Practice Brahmā King said to the Buddha: "This is unprecedented, O World-Honored One! Having attained the equivalence of all the dharmas, the Tathāgata manifests it to sentient beings by means of these wondrous form bodies." The Buddha said, "Brahmā king, all this has been accomplished through the power of my fundamental practice of the Śūraṅgama Samādhi. It is thus that the Tathāgata has attained the equivalence of all dharmas and has used these wondrous form bodies to manifest [this teaching] to sentient beings." When the Tathāgata explained this Dharma, Equivalent Practice Brahmā King and ten thousand Brahmā gods all achieved a pliant forbearance of all the dharmas. The Tathāgata then reined in his divine power, and the many Buddhas and seats all disappeared, so that the entire assembly saw only one Buddha.

At that time the Buddha told Resolute Mind Bodhisattva, "The Śūraṅgama Samādhi cannot be attained by Bodhisattvas of the first, second, third, fourth, fifth, sixth, seventh, eighth, or ninth stage. Only Bodhisattvas who are on the tenth stage can attain this Śūraṅgama Samādhi. What is the Śūraṅgama Samādhi? (1) It is to cultivate the mind as if it were like space. (2) It is to observe the present mental states [*hsin*] of sentient beings. (3) It is to discriminate the inherent abilities of sentient beings. (4) It is to comprehend the causes and results of sentient beings definitively. (5) It is to know that there is no karmic retribution within the various karmas. (6) It is to enter the various types of desire, without forgetting after entering. (7) It is to know firsthand the various types of natures. (8) It is always to be able to disport in the Flower Sound Samādhi, to be able to demonstrate to sentient beings the Adamantine Mind Samādhi, and to have autonomous mastery of all samādhis at will. (9) It is to see universally all the paths that beings traverse. (10) It is to attain unhindered knowledge of past karma. (11) It is for one's divine eye to be unobstructed. (12) It is to attain extinction of the outflows and not to realize any improper occasion. (13) It is to attain the wisdom of equivalent entering into both form and the formless. (14) It is to manifest
631b disportment in all of form. (15) It is to understand all sounds to resemble the characteristics of echoes. (16) It is to enter directly into the wisdom of mindfulness. (17) It is to make sentient beings happy with excellent speech. (18) It is to preach the Dharma according to the occasion. (19) It is to understand the proper and improper times. (20) It is to be able to transform the various roots. (21) It is to preach the Dharma without falsehood. (22) It is to

enter directly into the True. (23) It is to be able to subjugate well the [different] classes of sentient beings. (24) It is to be sufficient in all the Perfections. (25) It is to be without differentiation in one's deportment of going and stopping. (26) It is to destroy the various types of rational thought and false discrimination. (27) It is to exhaust the limits of the dharma-natures without destroying them. (28) It is to manifest bodies in the locations of all the Buddhas simultaneously. (29) It is to be able to maintain all the Dharmas preached by the Buddha. (30) It is to create physical manifestations autonomously, like shadows, throughout all the worlds. (31) It is to preach well the Vehicles for saving sentient beings and to protect the Triple Jewel always and unceasingly. (32) It is to generate great ornamentations throughout the entire future without one's mind ever having the thought of fatigue. (33) It is always to be able to manifest bodies in all the places where [sentient beings] are born, without stopping at any time. (34) It is to manifest activities wherever one is born. (35) It is to be able to fulfill well [the roles of] all sentient beings. (36) It is to be able to understand all sentient beings well. (37) It is for the teachings of the two [Hīnayāna] Vehicles to be immeasurable. (38) It is to be able well and completely to know the myriad sounds. (39) It is to be able to cause all the myriad Dharmas to flourish brightly. (40) It is to be able to make one eon be immeasurable eons. (41) It is to be able to make immeasurable eons be a single eon. (42) It is to be able to cause a single country to enter into an immeasurable number of countries. (43) It is to be able to cause an immeasurable number of countries to enter into a single country. (44) It is for limitless Buddha realms to enter into a single pore. (45) It is to manifest the entrance of all sentient beings into a single body. (46) It is to comprehend that the various Buddha lands are the same, like space. (47) It is for one's body to be able to pervade throughout the remainderless Buddha lands. (48) It is to cause all bodies to enter into the dharma-natures and to cause there to be no bodies at all. (49) It is to penetrate the characterlessness of all the dharma-natures. (50) It is to be able to comprehend all the expedient means

well. (51) It is to be able to penetrate all the dharma-natures with the one sound of the teaching. (52) It is to be able to expound on a single phrase of the Dharma for a countless number of immeasurable eons. (53) It is to contemplate well the differences among all the teachings. (54) It is to preach the Dharma knowing well [the occurrence of] agreement and difference [and the need for] abbreviation and dilation. (55) It is to know well how to pass beyond all the demonic ways. (56) It is to issue forth the refulgence of the great wisdom of expedient means. (57) It is to have wisdom as the primary [characteristic] of one's actions of body, speech, and mind. (58) It is to have supernormal powers always immediately available without [intentionally] practicing them. (59) It is to use the four unhindered wisdoms to make all sentient beings happy. (60) It is to manifest the power of the supernormal abilities to penetrate all the dharma-natures. (61) It is to be able to use dharmas of collocation to universally attract [*she, lit.* collocate] sentient beings [to the Dharma]. (62) It is to understand the languages of sentient beings in all the various worlds. (63) It is to have no doubts with regard to the phantasmagorical dharmas. (64) It is to be able
631c to maintain autonomous [freedom of action] throughout all the places of birth (*or,* generation). (65) It is to be without want for anything one needs. (66) It is to manifest oneself to all sentient beings autonomously. (67) It is [to understand] both good and evil to be identical to the fields of blessing. (68) It is to attain entry into all the secret dharmas of the Bodhisattvas. (69) It is always to issue forth a brilliant illumination throughout the remainderless worlds. (70) It is for one's wisdom to be immeasurably profound. (71) It is for one's mind to be like earth, water, fire, and wind. (72) It is to turn well the Wheel of the Dharma using the words and phrases of all the [individual] dharmas. (73) It is to be at the stage of a Tathāgata without obstruction. (74) It is to attain spontaneously the forbearance of the birthlessness of all dharmas. (75) It is to attain the real mind, which cannot be defiled by the impurities of the various afflictions. (76) It is to [be able to] cause all water to enter into a single pore without interfering with the nature of the

water itself. (77) It is to cultivate and accumulate the immeasurable blessed and meritorious good roots. (78) It is to know well all the expedient means for the transference [of religious merit to others]. (79) It is to be able to [perform] transformations well and to undertake universally all the practices of a Bodhisattva. (80) It is to have peace in one's mind about all the dharmas of the Buddha. (81) It is to have already transcended the body [generated from] one's own karma. (82) It is to be able to enter into the secret dharma-stores of the Buddhas. (83) It is to manifest disporting at will in the various desires. (84) It is to hear immeasurable dharmas and to maintain them sufficiently. (85) It is to seek all the dharmas without any feeling of satiation. (86) It is to be in accord with worldly conventions without being defiled thereby. (87) It is to preach the Dharma for people for immeasurable eons such that they all think [the time passed as if it were the interval] from morning to the [noon] meal. (88) It is to manifest various types of illness, lameness, deafness, blindness, and dumbness in order to save sentient beings. (89) It is to have a hundred thousand invisible *vajra* warriors always serving and protecting one. (90) It is to be able to contemplate naturally the enlightenment of the Buddhas. (91) It is to be able to manifest in a single moment of thought a life span of immeasurable countless eons. (92) It is to manifest all the elements of deportment within the two [Hīnayāna] Vehicles without internally dispensing with the practices of a Bodhisattva. (93) It is for one's mind to be well serene, empty, and without characteristics. (94) It is to manifest pleasure in the various amusements without internally dispensing with the Samādhi of the Remembrance of the Buddha [*nien-fo san-mei*]. (95) It is to be able to create innumerable sentient beings that may be seen, heard, or touched without disappearing. (96) It is to manifest the achievement of the enlightenment of Buddhahood in every moment of thought and to cause the attainment of emancipation in the teaching that proceeds from this basis. (97) It is to manifest entering a womb and becoming born. (98) It is to leave home and achieve the enlightenment of Buddhahood. (99) It is to turn the Wheel of the

Dharma. (100) It is to enter Parinirvāṇa without ever achieving extinction.

"Resolute Mind, thus does the Śūraṅgama Samādhi have the immeasurable ability to manifest all the supernormal powers of the Buddha, so that innumerable sentient beings may attain benefit thereby. Resolute Mind, the Śūraṅgama Samādhi cannot be understood by means of a single affair, a single condition, or a single meaning. All the meditations, emancipations, samādhis, autonomous supernormal powers, and unhindered wisdoms are all con-
632a tained within the Śūraṅgama Samādhi. It is likened to the currents from the mountain springs and rivers, which all enter the ocean. Thus are the Bodhisattvas' meditations all contained within the Śūraṅgama Samādhi. It is likened to the great valor of the Wheel Turning Sage King, which induces all the four types of soldiers to follow him. Resolute Mind, thus are the teaching of samādhi, the teaching of meditation, the teaching of discrimination, the teaching of emancipation, the teaching of *dhāraṇī,* the teaching of supernormal powers, and the teaching of brilliant emancipation: all these teachings are contained within the Śūraṅgama Samādhi. Hence when a Bodhisattva practices the Śūraṅgama Samādhi, he practices all the samādhis. Resolute Mind, it is likened to the seven treasures of the Wheel Turning Sage King, which follow him wherever he goes. Thus, O Resolute Mind, do all the Dharmas that contribute to enlightenment follow the Śūraṅgama Samādhi. It is for this reason that this samādhi is called Śūraṅgama (heroic march)."

The Buddha told Resolute Mind, "When a Bodhisattva resides in the Śūraṅgama Samādhi, he practices charity without having to seek for wealth [to donate to others]. All the treasures, food and drink, clothing, elephants and horses, and chariots within the great oceans, the heavens, and the realms of mankind within the great chiliocosm—all these objects are automatically given. All this is the achievement of the fundamental merit [of the Śūraṅgama Samādhi]. How much more so with the accomplishments performed at will through the divine power [of this samādhi]! This is said to be the fundamental fruit of the Perfection of Charity of the Bodhisattva residing in the Śūraṅgama Samādhi."

The Buddha told Resolute Mind, "When a Bodhisattva resides in the Śūraṅgama Samādhi, he is immovable in the precepts without having taken the precepts again. Because he wants to teach all sentient beings, he may manifest the maintenance of the precepts and the various rules of deportment. He may manifest violations and the elimination of transgressions, but his internal purity is always flawless. Because he wants to teach all sentient beings, he may be born in the realm of desire as a Wheel Turning Sage King, with a harem of princesses worshipfully surrounding him. He may manifest the existence of wife and children and may be wantonly engaged in the five desires, but internally he will always remain within meditation and the pure precepts, well comprehending the three disastrous transgressions. Resolute Mind, this is said to be the fundamental fruit of the Perfection of Morality of the Bodhisattva residing in the Śūraṅgama Samādhi."

The Buddha told Resolute Mind, "When a Bodhisattva resides in the Śūraṅgama Samādhi he completely cultivates the ultimate forbearance. Because of this, he cultivates forbearance before sentient beings are even born, he cultivates forbearance before the dharmas are even generated, he cultivates forbearance before the mind even takes form, he cultivates forbearance before [the discrimination of] self and other even occurs, he cultivates forbearance before there is even a thought of birth and death. He cultivates forbearance with the essence of Nirvāṇa, he cultivates forbearance without destroying the dharma-natures. Thus does the Bodhisattva cultivate forbearance without there being anything that is cultivated and without any not cultivating. In order to teach sentient beings, he is born in the realm of desire. He may manifest anger, but within he is pure. He may manifest the cultivation of distant transcendence, but [he knows that there actually] is no far
or near. In order to purify the sentient beings he may break worldly 632b
rules of deportment, but he never breaks the dharma-natures [never goes counter to the inner realities of things]. He may manifest

forbearance, but [in reality] there are no dharmas [that can be forborne]. He is able to forbear through the indestructibility of his permanent meditation. Thus does the Bodhisattva achieve forbearance. In order to eradicate the great anger of sentient beings, he always praises the blessings of forbearance, but he never attains either forbearance or anger. Resolute Mind, this is said to be the fundamental fruit of the Perfection of Forbearance of the Bodhisattva residing in the Śūraṅgama Samādhi."

The Buddha told Resolute Mind, "When a Bodhisattva resides in the Śūraṅgama Samādhi, he generates great energy and attains all the good dharmas, but he does not generate karma of body, speech, and mind. It is for the lazy that he manifests the practice of energy. He wants to make sentient beings follow my teaching, but he neither generates nor accepts the dharmas. Why? The Bodhisattva understands that all the dharmas completely and constantly reside within the dharma-natures, without coming and going. Thus does he distantly transcend the actions of body, speech, and mind; and yet he is able to manifest the practice of energy. Nor does he consider that dharmas achieve completion. He manifests the practice of energy within the world but is without any actions either within or without. He is always able to travel about the innumerable Buddha realms, but his body remains universally 'equivalent' and does not move. He manifests the practice of all the good dharmas but never perceives the good or wrong of any of the dharmas. He manifests the acceptance of teaching [from others] in his spiritual quest but never follows any teaching other than that of Buddhism. He manifests becoming intimate with the preceptors and masters but is revered by all gods and humans. He manifests earnest inquiries [about the teaching] but within himself has attained unhindered discrimination. He manifests reverence but is worshipped by all gods and humans. He manifests entry into the womb but is without defilement within all the dharmas. He manifests birth but does not perceive generation and extinction within all the dharmas. He manifests existence as a child but his physical faculties are all complete. He manifests abilities in the arts, medicine, magic, literature, mathematics, and the crafts but has already penetrated everything within himself. He manifests illness but has already permanently transcended the afflictions. He manifests old age, but his senses are already indestructible. He manifests death, but he has never been defeated by saṃsāra. Resolute Mind, this is said to be the fundamental fruit of the Perfection of Energy of the Bodhisattva residing in the Śūraṅgama Samādhi."

The Buddha told Resolute Mind, "When a Bodhisattva resides in the Śūraṅgama Samādhi, although he knows that the dharmas always have the characteristic of meditation, he manifests the various distinctions of meditation for sentient beings. He manifests residence in meditation in order to teach those with confused minds but does not perceive any confusion within the dharmas. All the dharmas are as the characteristics of the dharma-natures, and he subjugates his mind and is motionless in meditation. He manifests the various deportments of coming, going, sitting, and lying down, but he is always serene within meditation. He manifests agreement with what the majority say but never rejects the 632c
characteristics of the various meditations. Out of compassion for sentient beings, he enters the cities, villages, and countries, but he is always in meditation. He manifests eating, out of a desire to benefit sentient beings, but he is always in meditation. His body is hard, like *vajra*; inside it is substantial, not empty, and indestructible. Within it there are no growing organs or mature organs and none of the impure and malodorous defilements of defecation and urination. He manifests eating, but [the food] does not enter him. [He eats] only through his compassion to benefit sentient beings; although he has no faults in any of his [physical or sensory] functions, he manifests behavior like that of all ordinary people. However, he is actually without any activity that transgresses against the various [Buddhist] practices. Resolute Mind, when a Bodhisattva resides in the Śūraṅgama Samādhi he manifests no distinction between open space and villages. He manifests no distinction between living as householder or monk. He may manifest the white

robes [of the householder], but he is not lax. He may manifest [the form of] a monk, but he is not arrogant. He will not become a monk within the dharmas of the non-Buddhist teachings, so as to teach sentient beings. He is not affected by all the heterodox views, and he does not claim to achieve purity within them. He may manifest practice of all the non-Buddhist rituals, but he does not follow their practice of the path.

"Resolute Mind, he is likened to a guide who has led a group of people over a steep road, only to return to save other people. It is thus, O Resolute Mind, that the Bodhisattva residing in the Śūraṅgama Samādhi acts in accordance with the spiritual aspirations of sentient beings. [Sentient beings] may aspire to the path [i.e., the enlightenment] of the Śrāvaka, or the path of the Pratyekabuddha, or the path of the Buddha; he teaches them and leads them to salvation as appropriate, and then returns to save other sentient beings. Therefore he is called a guide.

"He is likened to a ferry, which carries innumerable people from this shore to the other shore. When it reaches the other shore it returns to carry over [i.e., save] more people. Thus, O Resolute Mind, does the Bodhisattva who resides in the Śūraṅgama Samādhi perceive sentient beings. He lets himself be carried along by the four currents of the river of birth and death only because he wants to help others escape. He accomplishes this according to the good roots sown by those sentient beings. If he sees that someone can be saved as a Pratyekabuddha, he manifests for that person the enlightenment of Nirvāṇa in his own body. If he sees that someone can be saved as a Śrāvaka, he preaches extinction to that person and enters Nirvāṇa together with him. Because of the power of the Śūraṅgama Samādhi, he manifests birth once again and saves more people. Thus is the Bodhisattva called the ferryman.

"Resolute Mind, he is likened to a magician who manifests his own death, dismemberment, and immolation before an audience. He may manifest to his audience that he is burned by fire and eaten by birds, but after receiving payment [from the audience] he will be revived. [The magician] is able to do so because he is proficient in magic. The Bodhisattva who thus resides in the Śūraṅgama Samādhi manifests old age and death in order to teach sentient beings, but actually there is no birth, old age, disease, and death. Resolute Mind, this is said to be the fundamental fruit of the Perfection of Meditation of the Bodhisattva residing in the Śūraṅgama Samādhi."

The Buddha told Resolute Mind, "When a Bodhisattva resides 633a
in the Śūraṅgama Samādhi, his senses are sharp in his cultivation of wisdom. Never perceiving the existence of the essences [*hsing,* natures] of sentient beings, he preaches the existence of sentient beings in order to save them. Never perceiving longevity [*shou*] and life span [*ming*], he preaches that there are [such things as] longevity and life span. Never perceiving karma and karmic retribution, he indicates to sentient beings that there are [such things as] karma and karmic retribution. Never perceiving the essences of the afflictions [*kleśa*] of saṃsāra, he preaches that one should understand the afflictions of saṃsāra. Never perceiving Nirvāṇa, he preaches that one proceeds to Nirvāṇa. Never perceiving the distinguishing characteristics possessed by the dharmas, he preaches that there are good and bad dharmas. Thereby is he able to carry [sentient beings] over to the other shore of unhindered wisdom. He manifests birth in the realm of desire but is not attached to the realm of desire. He manifests the practice of meditations of the realm of form but is not attached to the realm of form. He enters into the meditations of the formless [realm] but is born in the realm of form. He manifests the meditations of the realm of form but is born in the realm of desire. He manifests himself in the realm of desire but does not practice the practices of the realm of desire. He knows all the various meditations, and he knows the portions of meditation. He can freely enter into meditation and leave meditation. In order to teach sentient beings, he can be born anyplace at will. He is always able to accomplish the profound and wondrous wisdom and to eradicate all the various activities [*hsing, saṃskāra?*] of sentient beings. In order to teach sentient beings, he manifests the occurrence of activities, but he is actually without

activity with regard to the various dharmas. He has completely gone beyond all the various activities and has long since eradicated the illusions of self and personal possession, although he manifests the receipt of the various things that are required.

"When a Bodhisattva accomplishes wisdom such as this, everything that he does derives from that wisdom and is never defiled by the results of karma. In order to teach sentient beings he manifests being deaf and dumb, but subtle pure sounds actually occur within him. He comprehends the spoken word, the scriptures, and mathematics, and he does not have to stop to consider what Dharma to preach [on any given occasion]. Wherever he goes, audiences always consider his preaching wonderful, and he can always make [his listeners] be joyful and attain resolute [faith]. He preaches the Dharma as the occasion arises, and the wisdom of this Bodhisattva does not decrease.

"Resolute Mind, he is likened to men and women, who are either large or small, who carry vessels to a place where there is water, which may be a spring, a lake, a river, or the ocean. They fill the vessels large and small and return, but the various bodies of water do not decrease. Thus, O Resolute Mind, does the Bodhisattva who resides in the Śūraṅgama Samādhi appear to audiences anywhere, whether of kṣatriyas or brahmins, whether laypeople, monks, or gods. He appears to all these various congregations without any mental effort, and he is able to make them all joyous through his good words. He preaches the Dharma wherever it is appropriate to do so, but his wisdom is never lessened. Resolute Mind, this is said to be the fundamental fruit of the Perfection of Wisdom of the Bodhisattva residing in the Śūraṅgama Samādhi."

The Buddha told Resolute Mind, "When a Bodhisattva resides in the Śūraṅgama Samādhi, those sentient beings who see him all
633b attain emancipation. Those who hear his name, see his ritual deportment, hear him preach the Dharma, or see him in silence—all these attain emancipation. Resolute Mind, he is likened to the great medicine-tree king named Joyous Vision—all those who see him are healed of illness. Thus it is, Resolute Mind, with the Bodhisattva who resides in the Śūraṅgama Samādhi. The illnesses of greed,

anger, and stupidity of any sentient being who sees him will be eradicated. It is like the great medicine king named Eradication. If [this medicine] is painted on one's drums during wartime, the sound of the drum will pull the arrow, sword, or lance out and eliminate the poison from any injuries suffered from arrows, and the like. Thus it is, Resolute Mind, with the Bodhisattva who resides in the Śūraṅgama Samādhi. The arrows of greed, anger, and stupidity will naturally come out of those who hear his name, and the poison of wrong views will be completely eliminated, so that all the afflictions will operate no more.

"Resolute Mind, he is likened to the medicine tree named Sufficient. If a person uses its root, his illness will be healed. His illness will be healed by the stems, knots, core, bark, twigs, leaves, flowers, or fruit, which may be fresh, dried, or ground—any form may be used to heal the illnesses of sentient beings. The Bodhisattva who resides in the Śūraṅgama Samādhi is also like this. There is no time at which he does not benefit sentient beings—he is always able to eliminate all the afflictions. While preaching the Dharma, he concurrently practices the four embrasures [*she*] [charity, loving speech, beneficial action, and homologous behavior] and the various Perfections, so that [sentient beings] attain emancipation. Whether a person makes offerings or not, and whether there is benefit [to him] or not, the Bodhisattva always uses the advantage of the Dharma so that the person will attain peace. And when he dies and his body is eaten—whether by animals with two legs or four, or by birds, or by humans or non-humans—due to the power of the Bodhisattva's preceptual vows, when these sentient beings die they are reborn in heaven and are forever without the calamities of illness, pain, old age, and the afflictions. Resolute Mind, thus is the Bodhisattva who resides in the Śūraṅgama Samādhi like a medicine-tree."

The Buddha told Resolute Mind, "When a Bodhisattva resides in the Śūraṅgama Samādhi, for lifetime after lifetime he automatically understands the Six Perfections without having to study them from anyone else. Lifting his foot and lowering his foot, breathing in and breathing out, he is in possession of the Six Perfections with each moment of thought. Why? Resolute Mind, the entire body of a Bodhisattva like this is the Dharma, and his entire activities are the Dharma.

"Resolute Mind, he is likened to a king and his great ministers, who have a hundred thousand varieties of incense ground together into powder. If someone searches for one particular variety without having its fragrance mixed up with the other [varieties of] incense, Resolute Mind, within these hundred thousand varieties of incense powders, will he be able to separate one from the others?" [Resolute Mind answered,] "No, World-Honored One." [The Buddha continued,] "Resolute Mind, since the Bodhisattva has perfumed his body and mind with all the Perfections, he always generates the Six Perfections in every moment of thought.

"Resolute Mind, how can the Bodhisattva generate the Six Perfections in every moment of thought? Resolute Mind, the Bodhisattva has complete equanimity and is without attachment; this
633c is the Perfection of Charity [*dāna*]. His mind is well serene and ultimately without any wrong; this is the Perfection of Morality [*śīla*]. He understands that the mind exhausts [all] characteristics and exists unharmed within [the realms of] sensory data; this is the Perfection of Patience [*kṣānti*]. He strives in contemplation and selects [advantageous states of] mind but understands that the mind transcends characteristics; this is the Perfection of Energy [*vīrya*]. He is ultimately well serene and has controlled his mind; this is the Perfection of Meditation [*dhyāna*]. He contemplates the mind and understands the mind, penetrating the characteristics of the mind; this is the Perfection of Wisdom [*prajñā*]. Resolute Mind, a Bodhisattva who resides in the Śūraṅgama Samādhi possesses the Six Perfections in every moment of thought as given in this teaching."

At this time Resolute Mind Bodhisattva addressed the Buddha, saying, "Never before, O World-Honored One, [have I heard such a teaching]! The activities of a Bodhisattva who has achieved the Śūraṅgama Samādhi are inconceivable! World-Honored One, if the Bodhisattvas wish to practice the practice of the Buddhas, they should study this Śūraṅgama Samādhi. Why? World-Honored One, such Bodhisattvas manifest the practice of all the various activities of ordinary people, but in their minds they are without greed, anger, and stupidity."

At that time there was a great Brahmā king named Creating Sympathy within the audience. He addressed the Buddha, saying, "World-Honored One, if a Bodhisattva wishes to practice all the activities of ordinary people, he should study the Śūraṅgama Samādhi. Why? Such a Bodhisattva manifests the practice of all the various activities of ordinary people, but in his mind he is without the activities of greed, anger, and stupidity." The Buddha said, "Excellent, excellent, Creating Sympathy! It is as you have said. If a Bodhisattva wishes to practice all the activities of ordinary people, he should study the Śūraṅgama Samādhi, because he will not think about all that has to be learned."

Resolute Mind Bodhisattva said to the Buddha, "World-Honored One, if a Bodhisattva wishes to study the Śūraṅgama Samādhi, what should he study?" The Buddha told Resolute Mind, "It is likened to the study of archery, in which one first shoots at a large target. When one can hit the large target, one shoots at a small target. When one can hit the small target, one shoots at the bull's-eye. When one can hit the bull's-eye, one shoots at an [arrow]-shaft. When one can hit the shaft, one shoots at [a bundle of] one hundred hairs. When one can hit the one hundred hairs, one shoots at [a bundle of] ten hairs. When one can hit the ten hairs, one shoots at a single hair. When one can hit the single hair, one shoots at a hundredth of a hair. When one can hit a hundredth of a hair, he may be called a good archer. He [can shoot] unerringly and at will. Such a person can shoot without mental effort, with complete accuracy, on the basis of a sound heard in the dark of night, or if a human or nonhuman incautiously strikes at him.

"Thus, Resolute Mind, should the Bodhisattva who wishes to study the Śūraṅgama Samādhi first study the mind of ecstasy. After studying the mind of ecstasy, he should study the profound mind. After studying the profound mind, he should study great

sympathy. After studying great sympathy, he should study great compassion. After studying great compassion, he should study the four pure practices [*brahmavihāra*], which are sympathy, compassion, joy, and equanimity. After studying the four pure practices, he should study the five highest penetrations (the divine eye, the divine ear, clairvoyance, knowledge of others' past lives, and knowledge of anything at will), which have the highest benefit, always maintaining his mastery of them. When he has studied
634a the penetrations, he can then accomplish the Six Perfections. When he has accomplished the Six Perfections, he will be able to penetrate expedient means. When he has penetrated expedient means, he will be able to reside in the third pliant forbearance. When he can reside in the third pliant forbearance, he will attain the forbearance of the birthlessness of the dharmas. When he has attained the forbearance of the birthlessness of the dharmas, the Buddhas will confer the prediction of enlightenment on him. When the Buddhas have conferred the prediction of enlightenment on him, he will be able to enter the eighth Bodhisattva stage. When he has entered the eighth Bodhisattva stage, he will attain the Samādhi of Presence before the Buddhas. When he has attained the Samādhi of Presence before the Buddhas, he will never be without a vision of the Buddhas. When he is never without a vision of the Buddhas, he will be able to fulfill all the causes and conditions of the Buddhist Dharma. When he can fulfill all the causes and conditions of the Buddhist Dharma, he will be able to activate the merit of ornamenting the Buddha lands. When he can activate the merit of ornamenting the Buddha lands, he will be provided with a house and family into which to be born. When he is provided with a house and family into which to be born, he will enter a womb and be born. When he enters a womb and is born, he has fulfilled the tenth [Bodhisattva] stage. When he has fulfilled the tenth stage, he will then attain a title for his career as a Buddha. When he attains a title for his career as a Buddha, he will attain all the Bodhisattva samādhis. After he has attained all the Bodhisattva samādhis, he will be able to attain the Śūraṅgama Samādhi. When

he has attained the Śūraṅgama Samādhi he will be able to perform the affairs of a Buddha on behalf of sentient beings, but he will not dispense with the practices of the Bodhisattva. Resolute Mind, if a Bodhisattva studies the Dharmas like this, then he will attain the Śūraṅgama Samādhi.

"Once a Bodhisattva has attained the Śūraṅgama Samādhi, he has nothing more to study in all the Dharmas. Why? Because he has already well studied all the Dharmas. It is likened to being able to hit a portion of a hair [in archery], after which there is nothing more to be studied. Why is this? Because he has already studied [everything]. Thus it is, Resolute Mind, with the Bodhisattva who resides in the Śūraṅgama Samādhi. There is nothing more for him to study in all the Dharmas, because he has already studied all the samādhis and all the [forms of] merit."

At that time Resolute Mind Bodhisattva addressed the Buddha, saying, "World-Honored One, I will now explain a metaphor, to which I would beseech you to listen for a moment." The Buddha said, "Go ahead and speak." "World-Honored One, it is likened to a great Brahmā king of the trichiliocosm, whose contemplation automatically and effortlessly extends throughout the entire trichiliocosm. Thus is the Bodhisattva who resides in the Śūraṅgama Samādhi automatically and effortlessly able to contemplate all the Dharmas. Also, he is able to understand the minds and mental activities of all sentient beings." The Buddha told Resolute Mind, "It is as you have spoken. If a Bodhisattva resides in the Śūraṅgama Samādhi, he understands all the Dharmas of the Bodhisattvas and all the Dharmas of the Buddhas."

At that time there was in the audience an Indra king named Holding Mount Sumeru, who resided at the farthest extremity of the entire trichiliocosm. He addressed the Buddha saying, "World-Honored One, it is likened to living on the top of Mount Sumeru and being able to look at the entire world. Thus is the Bodhisattva 634b
who resides in the Śūraṅgama Samādhi automatically able to see the activities of the Śrāvakas, Pratyekabuddhas, and all sentient beings."

At that time Resolute Mind Bodhisattva asked the Indra king Holding Mount Sumeru, "Would you tell us from which of the four continents you have come? Where on Mount Sumeru do you reside?" The Indra king replied, "Good youth, a Bodhisattva who has attained the Śūraṅgama Samādhi would not have to ask where I reside. Why is this? For such a Bodhisattva, all the Buddha realms are his residence, yet he is not attached to any residence. He attains no residence and perceives no residence."

Resolute Mind asked, "Have you, sir, attained the Śūraṅgama Samādhi?" The Indra king replied, "Could the characteristics of 'attain' and 'not attain' exist within this samādhi?" Resolute Mind said, "No." The Indra king said, "Good youth, you should understand that when a Bodhisattva practices this samādhi, there is nothing that is attained in any of the dharmas." Resolute Mind said, "Since your understanding is like this, you must have already attained the Śūraṅgama Samādhi." The king said, "Good youth, I do not perceive that the dharmas have any place of residence. He who has no residence in all the dharmas has attained the Śūraṅgama Samādhi. Good youth, to reside in this samādhi is to be completely without residence in all the dharmas. If one is without residence, then one is without grasping. If one is without grasping, one is also without preaching."

At this time the Buddha said to Resolute Mind Bodhisattva, "Do you see the Indra king Holding Mount Sumeru?" "I do, World-Honored One." "Resolute Mind, this Indra king has automatically and of his own will attained the Śūraṅgama Samādhi. Residing in this samādhi, he is able to manifest himself in all the palaces for Indra kings throughout the trichiliocosm."

At this time the Indra king of this realm, Devendra, addressed the Buddha, saying, "World-Honored One, if Indra king Holding Mount Sumeru is able to manifest himself in all the palaces for Indra kings, why is it that I cannot see him in all the locations of the Indra kings?" At this time Indra king Holding Mount Sumeru replied to the Indra king [of this world system], saying, "Kauśika [Devendra], if I were to reveal my real body to you now, you would no longer take joy in your palace. I am always in the palace in which you reside, but you do not see me."

At this time Devendra addressed the Buddha, saying, "World-Honored One, I wish to see the wondrous body achieved by this Bodhisattva." The Buddha said, "Kauśika [Devendra], do you wish to see it?" "World-Honored One, I beseech you to let me see it." The Buddha said to Indra king Holding Mount Sumeru, "Good youth, reveal your true, wondrous body to this Indra king." Indra king [Holding Mount Sumeru] then manifested his true, wondrous body. At that time, the bodies of all the Indra gods, Brahmā gods, and world-protecting kings, Śrāvakas, and Bodhisattvas within the audience who had not attained the Śūraṅgama Samādhi became invisible, as if they were a collection of ink spots. The body of Indra 634c
king Holding Mount Sumeru became tall and imposing, like Mount Sumeru, the king of mountains itself, with brilliant light shining into the distance. At that time the body of the Buddha became even brighter and more apparent.

The Indra king Devendra addressed the Buddha, saying, "Never before, World-Honored One, [have I experienced such a thing as this]! The body of this Bodhisattva is unmatchably pure and wondrous. And the bodies of all the Indra gods, Brahmā gods, and world-protecting kings have all become invisible, like a collection of ink spots. World-Honored One, when I in the Hall of Good Wonders atop Mount Sumeru put on the Śakrābhilagna maṇi pearl necklace, the brilliance of it is such that the bodies of the entire assembly of gods become invisible. But I have now become invisible through the brilliant light of this Bodhisattva, and there is also no light from the precious necklace I am wearing!"

The Buddha told the Indra king Devendra, "Kauśika, even if the entire trichiliocosm were filled with Śakrābhilagna maṇi pearls, the brightly shining maṇi pearls of all the gods would render the [Śakrābhilagna] pearls invisible. Kauśika, even if the entire trichiliocosm were filled with the brightly shining maṇi pearls of all the gods, there is yet a bright adamantine maṇi pearl that can render all the other pearls invisible. Kauśika, even if the entire trichiliocosm were filled with bright adamantine maṇi pearls, there is yet a maṇi pearl embodying all the brilliances that can render the other pearls invisible. Kauśika, do you see the maṇi pearl embodying all the brilliances worn by this king?" [Devendra replied,] "I see it, World-Honored One. But the brilliance of this pearl is so intense my eyes cannot stand it." The Buddha told Devendra, "Bodhisattvas who attain the Śūraṅgama Samādhi may become Indra kings who always wear maṇi pearl necklaces such as this."

At this time the Indra king Devendra addressed the Buddha, saying, "World-Honored One, will those who have not generated the intention to achieve unsurpassable and perfect enlightenment on behalf of all sentient beings attain a pure and wondrous body such as this? Also, can one lose this Śūraṅgama Samādhi [after once attaining it]?"

At this time the god Gopaka [who had been the Buddha's princess Gopā before being born into the Heaven of the Thirty-three] said to the Indra king Devendra, "The Śrāvakas have entered into Suchness [*fa-i*, the stage of Dharma; i.e., entered into extinction], and although they have repeatedly extolled and delighted in the enlightenment of Buddhahood they cannot accomplish it. This is because they have created obstacles for themselves within saṃsāra. If a person generates the intention to achieve unsurpassable and perfect enlightenment on behalf of all sentient beings, he should generate it now as it should be generated. Such a person will love the path of the Buddha and will be able to attain the wondrous form body just revealed.

"It is likened to a person who is blind from birth. Although he may praise and love the sun and moon, he has never experienced their brilliant light. Thus it is with the Śrāvakas who have entered into Suchness. Although they extol and delight in the enlightenment of Buddhahood, the Buddha's merit has had no physical benefit for them. For this reason, those of great wisdom who wish to attain this wondrous body should generate the Buddha's
635a unsurpassable intention to achieve enlightenment. They will then be able to attain the wondrous body just revealed." When the god

Gopaka spoke these words, twelve thousand gods generated the intention to achieve unsurpassable and perfect enlightenment.

At this time, Resolute Mind Bodhisattva asked the god Gopaka, saying, "What merit should a woman cultivate to transform her body?" He answered, "Good youth, those who generate [the intention to achieve enlightenment in] the Mahāyāna do not perceive differences of male and female. Why? The mind of omniscience [*sarvajñā*] does not exist in the three realms. It is through discrimination that there is male and female. If your question is what merit a woman should cultivate to transform her body, then from the past she should serve the Bodhisattva(s) and be without deviation." [Resolute Mind asked,] "How should she serve?" [The god answered,] "As if serving the World-Honored One." [Resolute Mind inquired,] "What is it for one's mind to be without deviation?" [The god] answered, "Physical actions should follow oral actions, and oral actions should follow the mind. [When this is the case] it is said that the woman's mind is without deviation."

[Resolute Mind] asked, "How is the female body transformed?" [The god] answered, "As it is formed." [Resolute Mind asked,] "What does 'as it is formed' mean?" [The god answered,] "As it is transformed." [Resolute Mind] asked, "O god, what do you mean?" [The god] answered, "Good youth, within all the dharmas, there is no forming, no transforming. All the dharmas have one taste [i.e., emptiness, or Suchness], which is known as the taste of the Dharma. Good youth, through my vows I had the body of a woman. Even if I had wanted my body to be transformed into that of a man, the characteristics of the female body would have been neither destroyed nor dispensed with. Good youth, for this reason you should understand that male and female are both misconceptions. All the dharmas and misconceptions ultimately transcend these two characteristics."

Resolute Mind Bodhisattva asked Gopaka, "Do you understand some small part of this Śūraṅgama Samādhi?" [Gopaka] answered, "Good youth, what I know has been gained from others; I have not realized it myself. I remember one clear night in the past when

Śākyamuni Buddha was a Bodhisattva in the house of King Śuddhodana, when he was in the palace among the princesses. At that time Brahmā kings as numerous as the sands of the River Ganges came from the East [to receive his teachings]. Some of them inquired about the Bodhisattva Vehicle; some of them inquired about the Śrāvaka Vehicle, and the Bodhisattva answered each of them according to their questions. Within this group, one of the Brahmā kings did not understand the expedient means practiced by Bodhisattvas. He spoke as follows: 'If you are so wise, please answer my questions. How can you lust for royal rank and sensual pleasures [*lit.,* sensual desire]?' The other Brahmā kings, who comprehended the Bodhisattva's wisdom and expedient means, spoke to this one Brahmā king, saying, 'The Bodhisattva does not lust for royal rank or sensual pleasure. In order to teach sentient beings and [bring them to the ultimate] accomplishment, he has manifested himself as a Bodhisattva residing in the home. At present, in other locations, he has accomplished the enlightenment of Buddhahood and is turning the wondrous Wheel of the Dharma.' Upon hearing this, the first Brahmā [king] spoke as follows: 'What samādhi has he attained that makes him autonomously capable of such divine transformations?' The other Brahmā [kings] said to him, 'It is the power of the Śūraṅgama Samādhi.'"

635b [Gopaka continued,] "Good youth, at that time I thought as follows: 'When a Bodhisattva resides in samādhi, his divine power is able to respond in ways that are unprecedented. He may reside within desires and may administer affairs of state, but he never departs from his samādhi.' When I heard this [dialogue between the Brahmā kings], my reverence doubled, and there, at the Bodhisattva's [palace], I generated the thought of the World-Honored One, as well as the profound intention to seek unsurpassable and perfect enlightenment. [I vowed,] 'I hope that in the future I will be able to create merit such as this.' Good youth, that which I have perceived is only this small portion. All I know is that this Śūraṅgama Samādhi has a power for merit that is immeasurable and inconceivable."

Resolute Mind said to the Buddha, "How rare, World-Honored One, for someone to speak as profoundly as has the god Gopaka! This is entirely the accomplishment of the Tathāgata, because he has always been protected by spiritual compatriots. World-Honored One, not long from now the god Gopaka will certainly reside in the Śūraṅgama Samādhi and attain an autonomous power of divine transformations identical to that of the Tathāgata."

Resolute Mind Bodhisattva addressed the Buddha, saying, "World-Honored One, are there others within this assembly who have attained the Śūraṅgama Samādhi?" At that time there was a god in the assembly called Manifest Mind, who said to Resolute Mind Bodhisattva, "You are like a stupid traveling businessman who enters the ocean, saying, 'Are there any maṇi pearls within this ocean that I can take with me?' Your words resemble this. Why? Within this assembly of the great ocean of the Tathāgata's wisdom there are Bodhisattvas who have created the Dharma-treasure and who have generated great ornamentation [of it], and yet you sit here and ask such a question as 'Are there others within this assembly who have attained the Śūraṅgama Samādhi?'!

"Resolute Mind, there are within this assembly Bodhisattvas who have attained the Śūraṅgama Samādhi and who manifest the bodies of Indra gods, who manifest the bodies of Brahmā kings, who manifest the bodies of gods, dragons, *yakṣa*s, *gandharva*s, *asura*s, *garuḍa*s, *kiṃnara*s, and *mahoraga*s. There are those who have attained the Śūraṅgama Samādhi who manifest the bodies of monks and nuns and male and female novices. There are those who have attained the Śūraṅgama Samādhi who manifest bodies ornamented by themselves with the various auspicious physical marks [of enlightened beings]. In order to teach sentient beings, there are Bodhisattvas who manifest themselves in the bodies and forms of women, or who manifest themselves in the bodies and forms of Śrāvakas, or who manifest themselves in the bodies and forms of Pratyekabuddhas.

"Resolute Mind, the Tathāgata has the autonomous ability to manifest himself in any body and form, according to the manner

of the group he is teaching: kṣatriyas, brahmins, laypeople, Indra gods, Brahmā gods, or world-protectors. You should understand that this is entirely the fundamental fruit of the Śūraṅgama Samādhi. Resolute Mind, when you see that the Tathāgata is preaching the Dharma somewhere, you should understand that
635c there are innumerable Bodhisattvas there whose great wisdom automatically generates great ornamentation, who operate autonomously within all the dharmas, and who accompany the Tathāgata whenever he turns the Wheel of the Dharma."

Resolute Mind Bodhisattva addressed the Buddha, saying, "World-Honored One, I now suggest that this god Manifest Mind has attained the Śūraṅgama Samādhi, since his wisdom discriminates without hindrance and his supernormal abilities are suchlike." The Buddha said, "Resolute Mind, it is as you have said. This god Manifest Mind resides in the Śūraṅgama Samādhi. He is able to preach thus because he has penetrated this samādhi."

At that time the Buddha said to the god Manifest Mind, "You may now manifest a small portion of the fundamentals of the Śūraṅgama Samādhi." The god Manifest Mind said to Resolute Mind, "Do you wish to see a small [portion of the] power of the Śūraṅgama Samādhi?" [Resolute Mind] answered, "O god, I would like to see it." Since the god Manifest Mind had well attained the power of the Śūraṅgama Samādhi, he manifested transformations so that everyone in the assembly was adorned with the thirty-two marks of Wheel Turning Sage Kings, each with attendants carrying the seven precious things. The god asked, "What do you see?" Resolute Mind replied, "I see that everyone in the assembly is adorned with the physical marks of Wheel Turning Sage Kings, each with attendants carrying the seven precious things."

At that time the god manifested everyone in the assembly as Indra kings within Kauśika's Palaces of the Thirty-three, where a hundred thousand goddesses danced around them for their pleasure. Then again, using his divine power, he made everyone in the assembly take on the physical characteristics and deportment of Brahmā kings, residing in Brahmā palaces and practicing the four unlimited states [i.e., the *brahmavihāras*]. He asked Resolute Mind once again, "What do you see?" [Resolute Mind] answered, "O god, I see everyone in the assembly [in the form of] Brahmā kings." Then [the god] manifested his divine power once again, making everyone in the assembly take on the physical appearance of the elder Mahākāśyapa, holding his robe and bowl, entering into various meditations, and practicing the eight emancipations, without any [manifestation] differing [from the others in appearance]. He again manifested his divine power, making everyone in the assembly take on the physical characteristics and deportment of the Buddha Śākyamuni, each surrounded by monks and attendants. He asked again, "Resolute Mind, what do you see?" [Resolute Mind] answered, "O god, I see that everyone in the assembly has taken on the physical characteristics and deportment of the Buddha Śākyamuni, each surrounded by monks and attendants."

The god Manifest Mind said to Resolute Mind, "Such is the inherent power of the Śūraṅgama Samādhi. When a Bodhisattva attains the Śūraṅgama Samādhi, Resolute Mind, he is able to insert the trichiliocosm into a mustard seed, with the mountains, rivers, sun, moon, and stars appearing unchanged, and to manifest all this to all sentient beings without frightening them. Resolute Mind, such is the inconceivable power of the Śūraṅgama Samādhi!"

At that time the great disciples, along with the gods, dragons, *yakṣas*, *gandharvas*, Indra gods, Brahmā gods, and world-protect- 636a
ing kings all addressed the Buddha in unison, saying, "World-Honored One, the merit of him who attains the Śūraṅgama Samādhi is inconceivable. Why? Such a person achieves the ultimate enlightenment of Buddhahood and accomplishes the various brilliances [*ming, vidyā*] of wisdom and the supernormal powers. While sitting here today we have seen this assembly in various physical forms and several different transformations, and [after] consideration [we suggest] that those who have not heard of the Śūraṅgama Samādhi must be understood as being controlled by Māra. [On the other hand,] you must understand that those who have heard [of the Śūraṅgama Samādhi] are protected by the

Buddhas. How much more so for those who hear it and are able to practice it as preached!

"World-Honored One, if a Bodhisattva wants to penetrate the Dharma of the Buddha and reach the other shore [of Nirvāṇa], he should singlemindedly listen to [this teaching of] the Śūraṅgama Samādhi, then he should remember it, recite it, and preach it to others. World-Honored One, if a Bodhisattva wishes to manifest all the physical forms and deportments, he should comprehensively understand all the activities [*hsing, saṃskāra*] of the minds and mental attributes of sentient beings. Also, if he wants to understand comprehensively how to apply medicine to all the illnesses of sentient beings, he should listen well to the Dharma-treasure of this samādhi, then remember and recite it. World-Honored One, one should realize that if a person attains this Śūraṅgama Samādhi, he will enter into the realm of the Buddhas, with wisdom autonomous."

The Buddha said, "It is so, it is so. It is as you have spoken! He who has not attained the Śūraṅgama Samādhi cannot be called a Bodhisattva of profound practice. The Tathāgata would not describe such a person as sufficient in charity, morality, forbearance, energy, meditation, and wisdom. For this reason, if all of you wish to practice all the paths, you should study this Śūraṅgama Samādhi. You should not think about all the teachings to be learned."

At this time Resolute Mind Bodhisattva asked the god Manifest Mind, saying, "If a Bodhisattva wishes to attain this samādhi, what dharmas should he cultivate?" The god replied, "If a Bodhisattva wishes to attain this samādhi, he should cultivate the dharmas of ordinary people. If he perceives the dharmas of ordinary people, the dharmas of the Buddha will be neither conjoined nor dispersed. This is called cultivation of the Śūraṅgama Samādhi." Resolute Mind asked, "What conjoining and dispersing are there in the dharmas of the Buddha?" The god answered, "Conjoining and dispersing do not exist even in the dharmas of ordinary people, how much less so in the dharmas of the Buddha!" [Resolute Mind asked,] "What is cultivation?" [The god answered,] "To be able to penetrate [the fact] that there is no difference between the dharmas of ordinary people and the dharmas of the Buddha is called cultivation. But in fact, there is neither conjoining nor dispersing in these dharmas. Good youth, this is because there is no characteristic of birthlessness in all collocations of dharmas, because there is no characteristic of disintegration in all collocations of dharmas, because all collocations of dharmas have the characteristic of emptiness, and because there is no characteristic of acceptance in all collocations of dharmas."

Resolute Mind Bodhisattva asked again, "To what locations does the Śūraṅgama Samādhi extend?" The god answered, "The Śūraṅgama Samādhi extends to the mental activities [*hsin hsing*] of all 636b
sentient beings, but it does not depend on the characteristic of grasping of those mental activities. It extends to all places of birth, but it is not defiled by those places of birth. It extends to the locations of the Buddhas in all the worlds, but it does not discriminate the Buddhas' extraordinary physical characteristics. It extends to all sounds and speech, but it does not discriminate the characteristics of words. It can reveal all the dharmas of the Buddha, but it does not extend to absolutely all locations. Good youth, if you ask to what locations this samādhi extends, [the answer is that] this samādhi extends to wherever the Buddha goes."

Resolute Mind asked, "To what locations does the Buddha go?" The god answered, "Since the Buddha is suchlike, his going is without going." [Resolute Mind] asked again, "Does the Buddha not go into Nirvāṇa?" [The god] answered, "All the dharmas are ultimately Nirvāṇa. Therefore the Tathāgata does not go into Nirvāṇa. Why? He does not go into Nirvāṇa because [he is] the essence of Nirvāṇa." [Resolute Mind] asked again, "Did the Buddhas of the past, who were as numerous as the sands of the River Ganges, not go into Nirvāṇa?" [The god] answered, "Were they born, these Buddhas as numerous as the sands of the River Ganges?" Resolute Mind said, "The Tathāgata has preached that these Buddhas, who were as numerous as the sands of the River Ganges, were born and then passed into extinction." The god said, "Good youth, the Tathāgata has not [ever] said that [even] a single person came into the world to bring great benefit and peace to sentient beings. What is [the Tathāgata's] meaning? Has the Tathāgata definitively attained [a realization that] sentient beings have birth and extinction?" [Resolute Mind] answered, saying, "O god, the Tathāgata has not attained birth and extinction in the dharmas." [The god said], "Good youth, you should understand that although the Tathāgata preaches that the Buddhas appear in the world, the characteristics of the Tathāgata are in reality without birth. Although he preaches that the Buddhas proceed to Nirvāṇa, the characteristics of the Tathāgata are really without extinction."

[Resolute Mind] asked again, "Have all the innumerable Tathāgatas [existing] at present attained enlightenment?" [The god] answered, "The Tathāgatas, the characteristics of whom are without birth and without extinction, have thus attained enlightenment. Good youth, there is no distinction as to whether the Buddhas have come into [the world] or whether they have entered Nirvāṇa. Why? The Tathāgatas have penetrated [the truth that] all the dharmas have the characteristic of extinction. Thus are they called Buddhas." [Resolute Mind] asked another question, "If all the dharmas are ultimately extinguished, how can the characteristic of Nirvāṇa be penetrated?" [The god] answered, "If all the dharmas are ultimately extinguished, this is identical to the characteristic of Nirvāṇa; and likewise with the penetration of that characteristic. Good youth, the Tathāgatas do not come into [the world] on the basis of birth, residing, and extinction. The absence of birth, residing, and extinction is called 'coming into [the world] of the Buddhas.'"

Resolute Mind asked, "Is it because you reside in the Śūraṅgama Samādhi that you are able to preach this way?" [The god] answered, "Good youth, what do you think? When the Tathāgata transforms himself into a human, in what dharmas does he reside while preaching?" Resolute Mind answered, saying, "He is able to preach by utilizing his divine power as a Buddha." [The god] asked again, "In what location does the Buddha reside when he transforms
636c himself into a human?" [Resolute Mind] answered, "The Buddha

transforms himself into a human while residing in the nondual supernormal powers." The god said, "Just as the Tathāgata resides in the non-residing dharmas while he transforms himself into a human, so does the human thus transformed also reside in the non-residing dharmas while preaching." Resolute Mind said, "If there is no place of residing, how can there be preaching?" The god said, "Just as there is no place of residing, so it is with preaching." [Resolute Mind] asked again, "How can a Bodhisattva be sufficient in the discriminative ability to preach pleasantly?"

[The god] answered, "The Bodhisattva uses neither the characteristic of self, nor the characteristic of other, nor the characteristic of Dharma, yet there is preaching. This is called being sufficient in the discriminative ability of joyous preaching. In accordance with such preaching of the Dharma, neither the characteristics of words nor the characteristics of the Dharma are extinguished. If one thus preaches without using dualities, this is called being sufficient in the discriminative ability of joyous preaching. Also, good youth, if the Bodhisattva does not dispense with the phantasmagorical characteristics of the dharmas and does not reject the characteristics of echoes among the sounds, this is called being sufficient in the discriminative ability for joyous preaching. Also, just as the letters, sounds, and words are without place, without location, without interior, and without exterior, but are based on a multiplicity of conditions and exist without any place of residing, so [in truth] are all the dharmas, which are without place, without location, without interior, and without exterior, and without any place of residing. The [dharmas] are without past, future, and present; they cannot be expressed with letters and words. They must be penetrated within oneself; yet there is preaching. This is called being sufficient in the discriminative ability of joyous preaching. It is likened to an echo. All the sounds are preached in accordance with the characteristics of echoes." Resolute Mind asked, "What is the meaning of 'in accordance with' [*sui*]?" [The god replied], "Good youth, the meaning of 'in accordance with' is 'in accordance with space.' Just as there is nothing that is in accordance with space, so is there nothing that is in accordance with the dharmas (or, 'with the preaching of the dharma[s]'). The dharmas are without comparison, without metaphors or similes. It is said to be 'in accordance with' in order that there [may appear to be the] attainment [of realization]."

At this time the World-Honored One praised the god, saying, "Excellent, excellent! It is as you have preached. Bodhisattvas should not become afraid regarding this. Why? If there were being 'in accordance with' there would be no attainment of unsurpassable and perfect enlightenment."

Resolute Mind Bodhisattva addressed the Buddha, saying, "World-Honored One, from which Buddha land did the god Manifest Mind come?" The god said, "Why do you ask?" Resolute Mind answered, "I would like to do reverence in the direction of that [land], since it is the location in which this Bodhisattva wanders and resides." The god answered, "One who attains this Śūraṅgama Samādhi will be personally reverenced by all the gods and people of all the worlds."

At this time the Buddha told Resolute Mind Bodhisattva, "The god Manifest Mind has come here from the Wondrous Joy world of Akṣobhya Buddha. There does he always preach the Śūraṅgama Samādhi. Resolute Mind, all the Buddhas never fail to preach the
637a Śūraṅgama Samādhi! Resolute Mind, this god Manifest Mind will achieve the enlightenment of Buddhahood in this Sahā world! He wishes to eradicate the five tainted wrongs [prevalent in] this [world], to teach sentient beings in the pure Buddha land, and he has come here in order to increase his practice of the Śūraṅgama [Samādhi]."

Resolute Mind said to the Buddha, "When will this god achieve the enlightenment of Buddhahood in this world? What will be his title? And what will be the name of his world?" The Buddha said, "After the extinction of a thousand Buddhas during this Good Eon, sixty-two eons will pass without a Buddha. There will only be a hundred thousand ten-thousand hundred-million Pratyekabuddhas [during this time]. The sentient beings during this period will plant good roots, so that [this god] will be able to achieve

Buddhahood after the end of these [sixty-two] eons. His title will be King Praised for Pure Brilliance Tathāgata. The world at that time will be named Pure Vision. At that time King Praised for Pure Brilliance Tathāgata will be able to make the minds of sentient beings attain purity. The [minds of the] sentient beings of that world will not be obscured by greed, anger, and stupidity, but will attain pure faith in the Dharma and will all practice good dharmas. Resolute Mind, the life of King Praised for Pure Brilliance Tathāgata will be ten short eons. He will emancipate sentient beings with the Dharmas of the Three Vehicles. Of these, the Śūraṅgama Samādhi will be attained by immeasurable and innumerable Bodhisattvas, who will gain the power of autonomy within the dharmas. At that time Māra and his followers will all cultivate the Mahāyāna and take compassion on sentient beings, and that Buddha land will be without the three lower modes of existence and the various difficult locations (the hells). It will be ornamented with purity, like [the far-off continent] Uttarakuru. It will be without demonic affairs and the heterodox views. After the extinction of that Buddha, the Dharma will reside for a thousand ten-thousand hundred-million years. Resolute Mind, this god will achieve the enlightenment of Buddhahood in a pure land such as this!"

At this time Resolute Mind Bodhisattva addressed the god, saying, "You will attain great benefit! The Tathāgata has conferred on you the prediction of unsurpassable and perfect enlightenment!" The god replied, "Good youth, to be without anything that is attained in all the dharmas is called 'great advantage.' To attain anything in the dharmas is no advantage. Good youth, for this reason you should understand that not to attain the dharmas is called 'great benefit'."

When this Dharma was preached, twenty-five thousand gods who had previously planted virtuous roots all generated the intention to achieve unsurpassable and perfect enlightenment, and ten thousand Bodhisattvas attained the forbearance of the birthlessness of all dharmas.

Fascicle II

Translated by the Kuchean Tripiṭaka Master Kumārajīva during the Later Ch'in [Dynasty]

At that time Śāriputra addressed the Buddha, saying, "World-Honored One, never before [has anything like this occurred]! You are now preaching the Śūraṅgama Samādhi, but Māra has not come to disturb us!" The Buddha told Śāriputra, "Do you wish to see what is troubling Māra?" [Śāriputra said], "I would like to see that." The Buddha then emitted from the space between his eyebrows a light [showing] the form of a giant person. The entire assembly saw Māra bound up five times over [i.e., with his two arms, two legs, and head bound] and unable to escape. The Buddha asked Śāriputra, "Do you see Māra bound up five times over?" [Śāriputra said], "I see him. Who has bound up Māra?" The Buddha said, "This [was done by] the divine power of the Śūraṅgama Samādhi. When the Śūraṅgama Samādhi is preached in any Buddha land, any demons there with an evil wish to impede [its preaching] will perceive their own bodies to be bound up five times over through the divine power of the Śūraṅgama Samādhi and the Buddhas. Śāriputra, wherever the Śūraṅgama Samādhi is preached, whether while I am in the world or after my extinction, any demons or followers of the demons and anyone else harboring evil intentions will be bound up five times over by the divine power of the Śūraṅgama Samādhi." 637b5

At that time the gods, dragons, *yakṣas*, and *gandharvas* in the assembly addressed the Buddha, saying, "World-Honored One, our minds are without doubt regarding this samādhi. We will not impede [its preaching], because we do not wish to see ourselves bound up five times over. World-Honored One, because of our reverence for this samādhi, we will all go and protect anyone who preaches this Dharma, so that the samādhi will then [inspire them to] generate the thought of the World-Honored One." The Buddha told the gods and dragons, "Because you [have pledged] to do this you will attain emancipation from the twelve bonds of [mistaken] views. What are these twelve? These are the twelve: the bond of the view of self, the bond of the view of sentient beings, the bond of the view of life span, the bond of the view of person, the bond of the view of eradication, the bond of the view of permanence, the bond of the view of personal action, the bond of the view of personal possession, the bond of the view of being, the bond of the view of nonbeing, the bond of the view of [discrimination into] this and that, and the bond of the view of the dharmas. You should understand that any sentient being who wishes out of anger to damage the Buddhist Dharma resides in these twelve bonds of [mistaken] views. If a person has faithful understanding and is obedient and not contrary [to the Dharma] he will attain emancipation from these twelve bonds of [mistaken] views."

Śāriputra then addressed the Buddha, saying, "World-Hon-
637c ored One, is Māra now able to hear you preach the name of the Śūraṅgama Samādhi, [as we can]?" The Buddha said, "He can hear it as well [as you can], but he is unable to come [to this assembly] because he is bound up." Śāriputra said, "Why do you not use your divine power to make Māra unable to hear the preaching of the name of the Śūraṅgama Samādhi?" The Buddha said, "Cease! Do not say that! Even if worlds as numerous as the sands of the River Ganges were filled with a great fire, anyone hearing the preaching of the Śūraṅgama Samādhi should [be able to] escape. Why? I say that merely to hear the preaching of the Śūraṅgama Samādhi is to attain great benefit, superior to attaining the four states of *dhyāna* or the four *brahmavihāras*. Śāriputra, because Māra can hear the preaching of the name of the Śūraṅgama Samādhi, there

now will form the causes and conditions for his escape from the entire predicament [*lit.*, all the affairs] of being Māra. If he is bound up but able to hear, he should also be able to attain emancipation from the twelve bonds of [mistaken] views. It is for this reason, Śāriputra, that evil persons of heterodox views who have entered the web of demons should be able to hear this Śūraṅgama Samādhi. How much more so those who are pure of mind and who joyfully wish to hear!"

At that time there was in the assembly a Bodhisattva named Practicing Nondefilement in Māra's Realm, who addressed the Buddha, saying, "Thus it is, World-Honored One. I should now manifest [myself] in Māra's realm and with my autonomous divine power cause him to reside in the Śūraṅgama Samādhi." The Buddha said, "As you wish." Practicing Nondefilement in Māra's Realm Bodhisattva then suddenly disappeared from the assembly and reappeared in Māra's palace, where he said to Māra, "Why do you not listen to the Buddha preaching the Śūraṅgama Samādhi? Innumerable sentient beings have generated the intention to achieve insurpassable and perfect enlightenment and are escaping your realms. They are also helping others to become emancipated and escape your realms." Māra replied, "I hear the Buddha preaching the name of the Śūraṅgama Samādhi, but I have been bound up five times over and am unable to attend. That is, my two arms, two legs, and head [are bound." The Bodhisattva] asked the Māra again, "Who has bound you?" Māra replied, "Just as I decided to go disrupt those listening to the [preaching of the] Śūraṅgama Samādhi, I was bound up five times over. Thereupon, I thought, 'The Buddhas and Bodhisattvas have great virtue that is impossible to disrupt. If I go, I will be myself destroyed, not simply [bound up and] kept in this palace.' When I had this thought, I was released from my fivefold bonds."

The Bodhisattva answered, "Thus it is that all ordinary persons, in their discriminative thinking, mistakenly grasp at characteristics, making themselves bound. Their bonds exist because they think actively and theorize argumentatively; their bonds exist

because they see, hear, perceive, and know. Here there actually is no being bound and emancipated. Why? Because the dharmas are without bonds and are fundamentally emancipated, and because the dharmas are without emancipation and are fundamentally without bonds, [therefore the dharmas] permanently possess the characteristic of emancipation, and [therefore sentient beings are permanently] without stupidity. The Tathāgata preaches the
638a Dharma using this teaching. Any sentient being who understands the meaning of this and energetically strives in order to achieve emancipation will attain emancipation from all bonds."

At that time there were in Māra's assembly seven hundred goddesses who scattered heavenly flowers, incense, and necklaces before Practicing Nondefilement in Māra's Realm Bodhisattva, and then said, "When will we attain emancipation from Māra's realm?" The Bodhisattva answered, "You will attain emancipation when you are able not to destroy your bonds to Māra." [They inquired,] "What are our bonds to Māra?" [He replied,] "The sixty-two [mistaken] views. If you do not destroy the [mistaken] views, you will attain emancipation from your bonds to Māra." The goddesses said, "How can you say that we will attain emancipation by not destroying our bonds to Māra?" [The Bodhisattva] answered, "The [mistaken] views are fundamentally without coming and without going. If you understand the characteristic of the non-coming and non-going of the views, then you will attain emancipation from your bonds to Māra. The [mistaken] views are neither being nor nonbeing, [so] if you do not discriminate being and nonbeing, then you will attain emancipation from your bonds to Māra. To be without views is the correct view, but such a correct view is not correct and heterodox. If [you understand] the Dharma to be not correct and heterodox, without action and without influence, then you will attain emancipation from your bonds to Māra. [If you understand that] these [mistaken] views are neither within, nor without, nor in any intermediate location, [and if] you thus do not think about the [mistaken] views any more, then you will attain emancipation from your bonds to Māra." On hearing this teaching, the seven hundred goddesses attained the forbearance of accordance [with the dharmas] and said, "We also should practice nondefilement in Māra's realm and save everyone who has been bound by Māra."

Practicing Nondefilement in Māra's Realm Bodhisattva then said to Māra, "Your attendants have generated the intention to achieve insurpassable and perfect enlightenment. What are you going to do?" Māra replied, "I am bound up five times over and do not know what to do." The Bodhisattva replied, "You should generate the intention to achieve insurpassable and perfect enlightenment, so that you attain emancipation from these bonds." Through their compassion for Māra, the goddesses then said in unison, "You should definitely generate the intention to achieve insurpassable and perfect enlightenment! Do not create thoughts of fear where there is peace! Do not create thoughts of suffering in the midst of happiness! Do not create thoughts of bondage in emancipation!"

Māra then decided to try deceit, saying [to the goddesses], "If you give up the intention to achieve enlightenment, I will then generate the intention to achieve enlightenment." Using the power of expedient means, the goddesses then said to Māra, "We have all given up the intention to achieve enlightenment. You should now generate the intention to achieve insurpassable and perfect enlightenment. If a single Bodhisattva generates the intention to achieve enlightenment, then all Bodhisattvas will have the same intention. Why? The minds [of Bodhisattvas] are without distinction; they are all universally 'equivalent' with regard to the minds of sentient beings."

Māra then said to Practicing Nondefilement in Māra's Realm 638b
Bodhisattva, "I will now generate the intention to achieve insurpassable and perfect enlightenment. Because of the good roots [of merit of this action], release my bonds!" When he finished saying this, he saw himself released from his bonds. Using his supernormal power, Practicing Nondefilement in Māra's Realm Bodhisattva then emanated a great brilliance, revealing his pure and wondrous body and illuminating Māra's palace. Māra saw that his own body was without brilliance, like an ink spot.

Two hundred goddesses within Māra's assembly, being deeply attached to lustful desire, generated a defiled feeling of love upon seeing the beauty of the Bodhisattva's body. They said, "If you could stay with us, we would all follow your teachings." Understanding that the past [karmic] conditions of the goddesses made them ready for salvation, the Bodhisattva created two hundred gods [for them] who were imposing in countenance and physically no different [from himself]. He also created two hundred Māra-defeating palaces with jewel-bedecked towers. The goddesses all saw themselves in these jewelled towers, and each said to herself, "I will share great pleasure through being with this Bodhisattva. I hope never to be able to satiate my lustful desires." All of them generated a profound reverence for the Bodhisattva, who then preached the Dharma for them according to their needs, so that they all generated the intention to achieve insurpassable and perfect enlightenment.

At that time Practicing Nondefilement in Māra's Realm Bodhisattva said to Māra, "You may approach the Buddha." Māra thought, "My bonds have been released, so I can approach the Buddha and disrupt his preaching of the Dharma." With his attendants all round, Māra then approached the Buddha and said, "World-Honored One, do not preach this Śūraṅgama Samādhi anymore. Why? When you preached this samādhi, my body was immediately bound up five times over. I beseech the Tathāgata to preach about something else." Resolute Mind Bodhisattva then addressed Māra, "Who released your bonds?" [He] answered, "Practicing Nondefilement in Māra's Realm Bodhisattva released my bonds." [Resolute Mind asked], "What did you do such that your bonds were released?" Māra answered, "I generated the intention to achieve insurpassable and perfect enlightenment."

At that time the Buddha told Resolute Mind Bodhisattva, "Because Māra generated the intention to achieve insurpassable and perfect enlightenment in order to have his bonds released, his intentions were not pure. Thus it is, Resolute Mind, that in the last period of five hundred years after my extinction there will be many monks who will generate the intention to achieve insurpassable

and perfect enlightenment for [their own] benefit and with impure intentions. Resolute Mind, you should observe the power of the Śūraṅgama Samādhi and the spirit of the Buddha's Dharma: monks, nuns, laymen, and laywomen who hear about this samādhi may generate the intention to achieve enlightenment lightheartedly, with a desire for [self-]benefit, or under the influence of some other person. I understand that such attitudes may form the causes and conditions for the generation of the intention to achieve insurpassable and perfect enlightenment. How much more so those who hear about the Śūraṅgama Samādhi and generate the intention to achieve insurpassable and perfect enlightenment with a 638c
pure mind! You should understand that such persons will attain the ultimate and definite [attainment, i.e., Buddhahood] within the Buddha Dharma!"

Resolute Mind Bodhisattva addressed the Buddha, saying, "World-Honored One, Māra has heard the preaching of the Śūraṅgama Samādhi and has generated the intention to achieve enlightenment in order to be released from his bonds. Will this also constitute sufficient causes and conditions [for attaining emancipation in] the Buddha's Dharma?" The Buddha said, "It is as you have spoken. Due to the fortunate causes and conditions of this samādhi and the causes and conditions of generating the intention to achieve enlightenment, in the future he will be able to reject all the demonic affairs, demonic practices, demonic deceit, and demonic trouble-making. From now on, he will gradually attain the power of the Śūraṅgama Samādhi and will accomplish the enlightenment of Buddhahood." Resolute Mind Bodhisattva said to Māra, "The Tathāgata has now conferred on you the prediction [of future enlightenment]." Māra said, "Good youth, I have at present not generated the intention to achieve insurpassable and perfect enlightenment with a pure mind. Why has the Tathāgata conferred this prediction on me? As the Buddha has said, karma proceeds from the mind, and retribution proceeds from karma. I myself have no intention of seeking enlightenment, so why has the Tathāgata conferred this prediction on me?"

Wishing to eradicate the doubts of those in the assembly, the Buddha then told Resolute Mind, "There are four types of predictions of enlightenment that are conferred on Bodhisattvas. What are these four? They are the prediction of enlightenment before the intention to achieve enlightenment has been generated, the prediction of the enlightenment of those who are about to generate the intention to achieve enlightenment, the secret prediction of enlightenment, and the prediction of enlightenment at the moment someone attains the forbearance of the birthlessness of all dharmas. These are the four. [This teaching] is only understandable to the Tathāgatas—the Śrāvakas and Pratyekabuddhas are all unable to understand it.

"Resolute Mind, what is it to confer the prediction of enlightenment before the intention to achieve enlightenment has been generated? There may be a sentient being who has wandered throughout the five modes of existence. He may be in the hells, he may be an animal, he may be a hungry ghost, he may be a god, or he may be a human, but if his senses are sharp and he takes pleasure in the great Dharma, the Buddha will know that he will generate the intention to achieve insurpassable and perfect enlightenment in a few hundred thousand ten-thousand hundred-million immeasurable eons. During those hundred thousand ten-thousand hundred-million immeasurable eons he will practice the Bodhisattva path, making offerings to several hundred thousand ten-thousand hundred-million *nayuta*s of Buddhas and teaching several hundred thousand ten-thousand hundred-million sentient beings, causing them to reside in enlightenment. Also, after several hundred thousand ten-thousand hundred-million immeasurable eons, he will attain insurpassable and perfect enlightenment, after which he will have such-and-such a title and have such-and-such a Buddha land. His life span and his congregation of Śrāvakas will be such-and-such. After his extinction the Dharma will remain for such-and-such a length of time." The Buddha told Resolute Mind, "The Tathāgatas are able to understand all such things, even in cases exceeding this one. This is called conferring the prediction of enlightenment before the intention to achieve enlightenment has been generated."

At that time the elder Mahākāśyapa came forward to address the Buddha, saying, "From now on, we should generate the thought 639a of the World-Honored One with regard to all sentient beings. Why? We do not have the wisdom [to know] which sentient beings have the roots of Bodhisattvahood and which sentient beings do not. World-Honored One, because we do not know such things, we might belittle such sentient beings, only to our own disadvantage." The Buddha said, "Excellent, excellent! Kāśyapa, you have spoken well. It is because of this that I have preached in the Sūtras that people should not falsely evaluate sentient beings. Why? If you falsely evaluate other sentient beings, it will be to your own disadvantage. Only the Tathāgatas should evaluate sentient beings and others. It is thus that the Śrāvakas and other Bodhisattvas should think of other sentient beings as Buddhas [*lit.*, generate the thought of a Buddha regarding sentient beings].

"Now to the prediction of the enlightenment of those who are about to generate the intention to achieve enlightenment. For example, there may be a person who has long planted meritorious roots and who has cultivated the good practices, who is diligent and energetic, with his senses sharp, taking joy in the great Dharma, with the mind of great compassion, and seeking the enlightenment of emancipation for all sentient beings. When such a person generates the intention [to achieve enlightenment], he will reside in the state of non-regression and enter the stage of a Bodhisattva. He will be counted among those [whose Buddhahood] is assured and will escape the eight situations in which it is difficult [to encounter the Buddha's teaching, i.e., rebirth in the hells, as a hungry ghost, as an animal, as a god, in the joyous continent of Uttarakuru, as a deaf or blind person, as one who has worldly wisdom, or before or after the lifetime of the Buddha]. When it is appropriate for a person such as this to generate the intention [to achieve enlightenment], the Buddha will confer on him a prediction of insurpassable and perfect enlightenment, with a title of such-and-such, with such-and-such a land, and a life span of such-and-such. For such a person, the Tathāgata will confer the prediction of enlightenment through understanding his mind. This is called generating the intention [to achieve enlightenment] and conferring the prediction [of future enlightenment].

"The secret conferring of the prediction [of future enlightenment] is for Bodhisattvas who are constantly diligent in seeking insurpassable and perfect enlightenment but who have not yet received the prediction. [Such a Bodhisattva] takes joy in the various types of charity; he takes joy in all [types of] charity. He has a firm understanding of the Dharma, maintains the precepts without omission, and generates profound ornamentation. He has great power of forbearance and empathizes with sentient beings. With diligence and energy, he seeks the various good Dharmas. He is never lazy in either body or mind, [as he strives as energetically] as if his head were on fire. He practices mindfulness in peace and is able to attain the four *dhyāna*s. He seeks wisdom joyfully and practices the enlightenment of Buddhahood. Long does he practice the Six Perfections, and he has the characteristic of achieving Buddhahood.

"The other Bodhisattvas, dragons, *yakṣa*s, and *gandharva*s of that time will all have the following thought: 'Such a Bodhisattva, who is diligent and energetic like this, is truly rare! How long will it take him to attain insurpassable and perfect enlightenment? What will his title be? What will his land be called? What will be the size of his assembly of Śrāvakas?' In order to eradicate the doubts of these sentient beings, the Buddha confers the prediction so that the entire assembly is able to hear it. Only the Bodhisattva himself is unable to hear it, because of the Buddha's divine power. All the other sentient beings are made to know the Bodhisattva's title as a Buddha, the name of his land, and the size of his assembly of Śrāvakas. All their doubts are resolved, and they think of him [*lit.*, generate thoughts regarding him] as a World-Honored
639b One, but the Bodhisattva himself does not know whether he has already received the prediction [of future enlightenment] or not.

This is the secret reception of the prediction [of future enlightenment] of Bodhisattvas.

"The present reception of the prediction [of future enlightenment] is for Bodhisattvas who have long accumulated good roots with unremitting [true] perception. Constantly cultivating pure practices and contemplating the emptiness of selflessness, [such a Bodhisattva] attains the forbearance of the birthlessness of all dharmas. Knowing that such a person's virtue and wisdom are sufficient, the Buddha confers the prediction [of future enlightenment] upon him in the presence of a great assembly of all the gods, humans, demons, Brahmā gods, monks, and brahmins, saying, 'Good youth, you will attain Buddhahood after passing through several hundred thousand ten-thousand hundred-million eons. Your title will be such-and-such. Your land will be such-and-such. Your congregation of Śrāvakas and your longevity will be such-and-such.' At that time innumerable people will be inspired by his example to generate the intention to achieve insurpassable and perfect enlightenment. After receiving the prediction [of future enlightenment] in the presence of the Buddha, the Bodhisattva's body will ascend into space, to the height of seven *tāla* trees. Resolute Mind, this is called the fourth, or receiving the prediction in the presence."

Resolute Mind Bodhisattva then addressed the Buddha, saying, "Are there any Bodhisattvas in the present assembly who have received the prediction [of future enlightenment] in these four ways?" The Buddha answered, "There are." [Resolute Mind asked], "World-Honored One, who are they?" The Buddha said, "Lion King Bodhisattva, son of the layman Enjoys Desires, received the prediction [of future enlightenment] before he generated the intention [to achieve enlightenment]. In the same fashion, innumerable Bodhisattvas of other worlds have received the prediction [of future enlightenment] before they generated the intention [to achieve enlightenment]. There are also Serene Extinction Bodhisattva, Dharma Prince Great Merit Bodhisattva, Dharma Prince Mañjuśrī Bodhisattva, and innumerable other Bodhisattvas, upon whom the prediction [of future enlightenment] was conferred when they were ready to generate the intention [to achieve enlightenment]. They all reside at the stage of non-regression. Here also are Wise Valiance Bodhisattva and Beneficial Mind Bodhisattva. There are innumerable Bodhisattvas like them, who have had the prediction [of future enlightenment] conferred on them secretly. Resolute Mind, I, Maitreya, and all the thousand Bodhisattvas of this Wisdom Eon all attained the forbearance of the birthlessness of all dharmas and received the prediction [of future enlightenment] in the presence [of a Buddha]."

Resolute Mind addressed the Buddha, saying, "How rare, World-Honored One! The practices of the Bodhisattvas are inconceivable! Their receipt of the prediction [of future enlightenment] is also inconceivable! The Śrāvakas and Pratyekabuddhas are all unable to understand this; how much more so the other sentient beings!" The Buddha said, "Resolute Mind, the energy and divine powers practiced and generated by Bodhisattvas are all inconceivable."

At that time the goddesses taught by Practicing Nondefilement in Māra's Realm Bodhisattva and made to generate the intention to achieve insurpassable and perfect enlightenment all scattered heavenly flowers above the Buddha and addressed him, saying, "World-Honored One, we do not wish to receive a prediction [of our future enlightenment] secretly. We wish to attain the forbearance of the birthlessness of all dharmas and receive the prediction [of future enlightenment] in your presence. We beseech you, World-
639c Honored One, to grant us a prediction of insurpassable and perfect enlightenment now!"

The Buddha smiled delicately, and from his mouth appeared a wondrous refulgence of variegated colors that illuminated all the world and then returned to enter him through the crown of his head. Ānanda addressed the Buddha, saying, "World-Honored One, why do you smile?" The Buddha told Ānanda, "Do you now see these two hundred goddesses reverently holding their palms together in front of the Tathāgata?" [Ānanda replied], "I see them, World-Honored One." [The Buddha said], "Ānanda, these goddesses have already deeply planted good roots before five hundred Buddhas of the past. From this time forth they will make offerings to innumerable Buddhas. After seven hundred immeasurable eons, they will all achieve Buddhahood and have the titles of Pure King [such-and-such]. Ānanda, after the end of these goddesses' lifetimes, they will be converted to the form of [human] females and be born in the Tuṣita heaven, where they will make offerings to and serve Maitreya Bodhisattva."

At that time, when Māra heard that the goddesses had already received a prediction [of future enlightenment], he addressed the Buddha, saying, "World-Honored One, I am now unable to exercise autonomy over my own attendants, because [they] have heard you preach the Śūraṅgama Samādhi. How much less [my power over] others who have also heard! If a person is able to hear the [preaching of the] Śūraṅgama Samādhi, he will definitely attain residence within the Buddha's Dharma."

The goddesses then spoke fearlessly to Māra, saying, "You should not lament so. We have not now left your realm. Why? Māra's realm is suchlike, just as the realm of the Buddhas is suchlike. The Suchness of Māra's realm and the Suchness of the realm of the Buddhas are identical and not separate, and we will not transcend this Suchness. The characteristics of Māra's realm are the characteristics of the realm of the Buddhas. The dharmas of Māra's realm and the dharmas of the realm of the Buddhas are identical and not separate, and we will not leave or escape this characteristic of the dharmas. Māra's realm is without any fixed dharmas that can be manifested; likewise is the realm of the Buddhas without any fixed dharmas that can be manifested. Māra's realm and the realm of the Buddhas are not different and not separate, and we will not leave or escape this characteristic of the dharmas. Therefore, you should understand that all the dharmas are indeterminate. Since they are indeterminate, you have no attendants and there are none who are not your attendants."

At that time Māra became despondent and distraught and wished to return to his heaven, but Practicing Nondefilement in

Māra's Realm Bodhisattva addressed him, saying, "Where do you wish to go?" Māra said, "I wish to return to the palace where I reside." The Bodhisattva said, "You may be in your palace without leaving this assembly," and Māra then saw himself within his own palace. The Bodhisattva said, "What do you see?" Māra replied, "I see myself within my own palace. The pleasant grove, garden, and lake are mine." The Bodhisattva said, "You may now donate them to the Tathāgata." Māra said, "So it shall be." When he said this he saw the Tathāgata, Śrāvakas, Bodhisattvas, and the entire great assembly within [the palace listening to the]
640a preaching of the Śūraṅgama Samādhi.

Ānanda then addressed the Buddha, saying, "World-Honored One, in the present location, [which has just been donated to you,] you are preaching the Śūraṅgama Samādhi. Previously, you attained enlightenment after being given food. Of the blessings received by the two donors, which is greater?" The Buddha said, "Ānanda, after food was given to me, I achieved insurpassable and perfect enlightenment. After I ate, I turned the Wheel of the Dharma. After I ate, I preached the Śūraṅgama Samādhi. There is no distinction among the blessings [derived from these] three [offerings of] food.

"Ānanda, where was I when I attained insurpassable and perfect enlightenment? You should understand that that location was the Vajrāsana. All the Buddhas of the past, future, and present attain the enlightenment of Buddhahood within [the Vajrāsana]. Wherever they are, they preach the Śūraṅgama Samādhi identically and without any difference. It is the same with the locations in which [the scriptures] are recited or copied. Ānanda, as to the offering of food to me prior to the first turning of the Wheel of the Dharma, if a Dharma master recites or preaches this Śūraṅgama Samādhi after receiving an offering of food, the blessings accruing from these two offerings will be identical and not different. Also, Ānanda, as to when I reside in the monastery and use the eighteen types of supernormal transformations to lead sentient beings to emancipation, if someone recites or preaches this Śūraṅgama

Samādhi in another monastery [after receiving an offering of food], the blessings accruing from these two offerings will be identical and not different."

Ānanda then said to Māra, "You have attained great benefit, since you have been able to donate your palace and have had the Buddha reside therein." Māra said, "This was the effect of the compassionate power of Practicing Nondefilement in Māra's Realm Bodhisattva."

Resolute Mind Bodhisattva addressed the Buddha, "World-Honored One, this autonomous mastery of divine power of Practicing Nondefilement in Māra's Realm Bodhisattva—is it due to his residence in the Śūraṅgama Samādhi?" The Buddha said, "Resolute Mind, it is as you have said. This Bodhisattva now resides in this samādhi and is thus able to have autonomous mastery of divine power. He manifests the practice of all the practices of Māra's realm, but is able to remain undefiled by those demonic practices. He manifests pleasure with the goddesses, but is actually never influenced by the evil dharmas of lust. This good youth resides in the Śūraṅgama Samādhi and manifests entry into Māra's palace, but his body never leaves my assembly. He manifests amusement in the pleasures of Māra's realm, but teaches sentient beings with the Dharma of the Buddhas."

Resolute Mind Bodhisattva addressed the Buddha, saying, "World-Honored One, you reside in the Śūraṅgama Samādhi and are able to manifest various types of autonomous divine power. How excellent this is, World-Honored One! Could you explain this briefly?" The Buddha said, "Resolute Mind, I am now residing in the Śūraṅgama Samādhi throughout the trichiliocosm: in the hundred hundred-million [worlds] beneath the fourfold heavens, the hundred hundred-million suns and moons, the hundred hundred-million places of the heavenly kings, the hundred hundred-million Heavens of the Thirty-three, the hundred hundred-million Yama heavens, the hundred hundred-million Tuṣita heavens, the hundred hundred-million Joyous heavens, the hundred hundred-million Autonomous Transformation of Others' [Pleasures] heavens,

etc., up until the hundred hundred-million Ultimate in Materiality
640b heavens, the hundred hundred-million Mount Sumerus, and the hundred hundred-million great oceans, [all of which] is called the trichiliocosm. Resolute Mind, I reside in the Śūraṅgama Samādhi throughout the trichiliocosm.

"I may manifest the practice of the Perfection of Charity in [this continent] Jambudvīpa, or I may manifest the practice of the Perfection of Morality in Jambudvīpa, or I may manifest the practice of the Perfection of Patience in Jambudvīpa, or I may manifest the practice of the Perfection of Energy in Jambudvīpa, or I may manifest the practice of the Perfection of Meditation in Jambudvīpa, or I may manifest the practice of the Perfection of Wisdom in Jambudvīpa, or I may manifest myself as an immortal god with the five supernormal powers in Jambudvīpa, or I may manifest myself as a householder in Jambudvīpa, or I may manifest myself as a monk in Jambudvīpa.

"I may manifest myself in the location of the penultimate birth in the Tuṣita heaven, or I may manifest myself as a Wheel Turning Sage King throughout [the world] beneath the fourfold heavens, or I may become an Indra king, or a Brahmā king, or one of the four heavenly kings, or the king of the Yama heaven, or the king of the Tuṣita heaven, or the king of the Joyous heaven, or the king of the Teaching Others Autonomy heaven. I may manifest myself as an elder, or I may manifest myself as a layman, or I may manifest myself as a minor prince or a great king, or I may become a kṣatriya, or I may become a brahmin, or I may become a Bodhisattva.

"Or, within [the world] beneath the fourfold heavens, I may wish to be reborn from the Tuṣita heaven into the world below and manifest entry into a womb, or manifest location in a womb, or manifest a desire to be born. I may manifest being born, walking seven steps, and raising my hand and saying, 'On earth and in the heavens, only I am worthy of honor.' I may manifest being in a palace, accompanied by princesses, or I may manifest leaving home, or I may manifest ascetic practices, or I may manifest taking grass [for a seat], or I may manifest sitting on the seat of enlightenment [*bodhimaṇḍa*], or I may manifest subjugating Māra, or I may manifest achieving Buddhahood, or I may manifest seeing the tree king [the god within the tree behind the *bodhimaṇḍa*], or I may manifest being asked by Indra and Brahmā to turn the Wheel of the Dharma, or I may manifest turning the Wheel of the Dharma, or I may manifest dispensing with my life, or I may manifest entering Nirvāṇa, or I may manifest having my body cremated, or I may manifest my entire body as relics, or I may manifest having my physical relics scattered [divided].

"I may manifest the imminent extinction of the Dharma, or I may manifest the extinction of the Dharma. I may manifest an immeasurable life span, or I may manifest a very short life span. I may manifest a land without the names of any evil modes of existence, or I may manifest the existence of the evil modes. I may manifest Jambudvīpa pure and ornamented like a heavenly palace, or I may manifest the evils, or I may manifest superior, intermediate, and inferior [realms].

"Resolute Mind, all this is [done through the] autonomous divine power of the Śūraṅgama Samādhi. When a Bodhisattva manifests entry into Nirvāṇa he does not undergo ultimate extinction but rather is able to manifest such an autonomous divine power throughout the trichiliocosm, manifesting ornamentations [of the Dharma] such as these. Resolute Mind, you see me now [in this world] underneath the fourfold heavens turning the Wheel of the Dharma, but elsewhere in Jambudvīpa I have not yet achieved Buddhahood, and yet elsewhere in Jambudvīpa I have already 640c
manifested entry into extinction. This is known as the teaching entered [by means of] the Śūraṅgama Samādhi."

At that time the various gods, dragons, *yakṣa*s, and *gandharva*s within the assembly, as well as the Bodhisattvas and great disciples, all had the following thought: "Is it only in this trichiliocosm that Śākyamuni Buddha has this divine power, or does he also have this power in other worlds?" Dharma Prince Mañjuśrī, knowing the thoughts of those in the assembly and wanting to eradicate their doubts, then addressed the Buddha saying, "World-Honored

One, in my wandering throughout the Buddha lands, I have been to a Buddha land that is more than sixty times as many worlds above our world as there are grains of sand in the River Ganges. The name of this Buddha land is Brilliance of a Single Lamp, and there is a Buddha there who preaches the Dharma on behalf of people. I went to him, reverenced him by placing my head on his feet, and asked, 'World-Honored One, what is your title? How should I address you as a Buddha?' The Buddha there answered me, 'You should proceed to Śākyamuni Buddha. He will answer you.' World-Honored One, if one were to speak of the merit and splendor of that Buddha land, one would not finish in an entire eon. Even more than this, that land lacks the names of Śrāvaka and Pratyekabuddha; there are only Bodhisattva monks, [to whom that Buddha] constantly turns the Wheel of the Dharma, preaching without [ever] regressing. I beseech you, World-Honored One, to please tell us the name of this Buddha, please tell us about the Buddha who is preaching the Dharma in the Land of the Brilliance of a Single Lamp!"

At that time the Buddha told Dharma Prince Mañjuśrī, "Listen well! Do not be afraid or have doubts! Why? The divine power of the Buddha is inconceivable. The power of the Śūraṅgama Samādhi is also inconceivable. Mañjuśrī, he who preaches the Dharma in the Land of the Brilliance of a Single Lamp is a Buddha with the title King of Brilliance That Autonomously Manifests All Merit. Mañjuśrī, the Buddha King of Brilliance that Autonomously Manifests All Merit of that Land of the Brilliance of a Single Lamp is actually [one of] my own bodies, which I have manifested in that land through my divine power as a Buddha. It is I who constantly turn the Wheel of the Dharma, preaching without [ever] regressing. This is a pure land cultivated by me in past lives. Mañjuśrī, you should now understand that I have this divine power throughout the immeasurable and innumerable hundred ten-thousand thousand hundred-million *nayuta*s of other lands. The Śrāvakas and Pratyekabuddhas are unable to understand this. Mañjuśrī, this is entirely the power of the Śūraṅgama Samādhi.

"The Bodhisattva always manifests his divine transformations in immeasurable worlds, but there is no movement or change in the samādhi [itself]. Mañjuśrī, it is likened to the sun and moon in their own palaces, which manifest all the cities, towns, and villages without ever moving themselves. Likewise does the Bodhisattva reside in the Śūraṅgama Samādhi: without ever moving himself, he is able to manifest his bodies throughout the immeasurable worlds, preaching the Dharma according to the pleasure 641a
of his congregations."

At that time those in the assembly had [an experience they had] never had before. They all jumped up in great and immeasurable joy, holding their palms together in reverence. The gods, dragons, *yakṣa*s, *gandharva*s, *asura*s, *garuḍa*s, *kiṃnara*s, and *mahoraga*s scattered pearl-flowers, wondrous flowers of variegated colors, incense powders, and unguents about above the Buddha, [meanwhile] performing the dances of their heavens and making offerings to the Tathāgata. The disciples took off their upper robes and offered them to the Buddha, and the Bodhisattvas then scattered about above the Buddha [a mass of] wondrously colored flowers the size of Mount Sumeru, as well as various types of incense powders, unguents, and jewelled necklaces, all saying, "Thus it should be, World-Honored One—if the Śūraṅgama Samādhi is preached somewhere, that place should be [as firm as] *vajra*. If someone hears the preaching of this samādhi, believes in it, recites it, and preaches it for others without their being shocked or afraid, it should be understood that such a person will have the forbearance of adamantine indestructibility. Profoundly residing in his faith, he will be protected by the Buddhas. Having extensively planted good roots, he will attain great benefit. Subjugating the demons and enemies, he will eradicate [the influence of] the evil modes of existence and will be protected by spiritual compatriots. World-Honored One, this is how we understand the doctrine that the Buddha has preached. If a sentient being hears this Śūraṅgama Samādhi and has faith in it, reciting it and understanding its doctrines, preaching it for people and practicing it according to how you have preached it, then such a person will reside in the Dharma of the Buddhas and will attain to the ultimately certain [attainment] without regressing."

The Buddha said, "Thus it is, thus it is. It is as you have said. There will be some who do not extensively plant good roots, and who hear the Śūraṅgama Samādhi but are unable to believe in it. There will be fewer who hear the Śūraṅgama Samādhi and are able to believe in it, and more who are unable to believe. Good youth, there are four types of persons who can hear and have faith in this samādhi. What are these four? The first are those who have heard this samādhi from the Buddhas in the past. The second are those who are protected by spiritual compatriots and who long for the enlightenment of the Buddhas. The third are those with good roots that are deep and wide and who love the great Dharma. The fourth are those who have themselves realized the profound Dharma of the Mahāyāna. These are the four types of persons who are able to believe in a samādhi such as this. Good youth, there are also Arhats who have completed their vows, those who believe and practice as they have been taught, and those who practice the Dharma according to their own understanding. Since these persons believe in and follow my words, they will believe in this samādhi but not realize it themselves. Why? This samādhi cannot be understood by any of the Śrāvakas and Pratyekabuddhas. How much less by other sentient beings!"

The elder Mahākāśyapa then addressed the Buddha, saying, "World-Honored One, it is likened to a person who is blind from birth. In his dreams he may see various forms with his eyes and be
641b greatly happy, and he may reside with and talk with sighted people in his dreams. When he awakes, however, he will not see form. We are like this: when we [disciples] had not heard of this Śūraṅgama Samādhi, our hearts were happy, and we declared that we had attained the heavenly eye. We resided together with the Bodhisattvas and spoke with them, discussing the doctrines. World-Honored One, now that we have heard of this samādhi from you [we realize that] we did not understand. Like people blind from birth,

we were unable to understand the Dharmas practiced by the Buddhas and Bodhisattvas. From now on, we will think of our former selves as if we had been blind from birth, with no wisdom regarding your profound Dharma and neither understanding nor [even] perceiving your practices. From now on we will understand that it was the Bodhisattvas who have really attained the heavenly eye and who have been able to attain such profound wisdoms. World-Honored One, if a person is without omniscience, how can he say 'I am wise, I am a field of blessings'?"

The Buddha said, "Thus it is, thus it is. Kāśyapa, it is as you have spoken. The Śrāvakas and Pratyekabuddhas are unable to attain to the profound wisdoms attained by the Bodhisattvas." When Mahākāśyapa spoke these words, eight thousand sentient beings all generated the intention to achieve insurpassable and perfect enlightenment.

Resolute Mind Bodhisattva then asked Dharma Prince Mañjuśrī, "Mañjuśrī, [Kāśyapa has just used] the term 'field of blessings'. What is a 'field of blessings'?" Mañjuśrī said, "Those who possess the ten types of practice are called fields of blessings. What are these ten? [They are] (1) to reside in the emancipations of emptiness, characteristiclessness, and wishlessness without entering into the absolute; (2) to understand the Four Noble Truths without realizing the fruit of enlightenment; (3) to practice the eight emancipations without dispensing with the practice of the Bodhisattva; (4) to be able to generate the three wisdoms and yet practice throughout the triple realm; (5) to be able to manifest the form and deportment of a Śrāvaka and follow the [Buddha's] oral teaching without seeking the Dharma from anyone else; (6) to manifest the form and deportment of a Pratyekabuddha and yet preach the Dharma with unhindered discrimination; (7) to remain constantly in meditation and yet manifest the practice of all the various practices; (8) never to depart from the correct path but to manifest entry into the heterodox paths; (9) to have profound greed and defiled lust but to transcend the desires and all the afflictions; and (10) to enter into Nirvāṇa and neither destroy nor dispense with saṃsāra. These are the ten. You should understand that a person [versed in the Śūraṅgama Samādhi] is a true field of blessings."

Resolute Mind Bodhisattva then asked Subhūti, "Elder Subhūti, the World-Honored One has preached that you are premier among the fields of blessings. Have you attained these ten?" Subhūti said, "I do not have even one of them. How could I have [all] ten?" Resolute Mind said, "Why are you called premier among the fields of blessings?" Subhūti said, "I am not premier among the fields of blessings in the context of the Buddhas and Bodhisattvas. The Buddha has preached that I am premier in the fields of blessings in the context of the Śrāvakas and Pratyekabuddhas. Resolute Mind, I
641c am like the princes of a marginal location who are called kings. If a Wheel Turning Sage King went to that marginal location, the princes would no longer be called kings—there would then be only that Wheel Turning Sage King. This is because the virtue of that Sage King is particularly wondrous and excellent. Resolute Mind, since there are places in the countries, cities, towns, and villages where there are no Bodhisattvas, I may be said to be a field of blessings in that context. However, where the Buddha and Bodhisattvas are, I may not be called a field of blessings. The Bodhisattvas possess omniscience and are therefore superior to me." At this time the Buddha praised Subhūti, saying, "Excellent, excellent. It is as you have spoken. These are the words of a great disciple who is without arrogance."

Resolute Mind Bodhisattva then asked Dharma Prince Mañjuśrī, "Mañjuśrī, you are said to be well-versed (*lit.,* greatly heard) [in the Buddhist scriptures]. Why are you called well-versed?" Mañjuśrī said, "To hear a single phrase of the Dharma, to understand within it the thousand ten-thousand hundred-million doctrines, and to explain it extensively for a hundred thousand ten-thousand eons, with one's wisdom and discrimination inexhaustible: this is called 'well-versed.' Also, Resolute Mind Bodhisattva, to listen to and be able to maintain [remember and recite] everything preached by all the innumerable Buddhas of the ten directions, so that there is not a single phrase one has not heard—so that every [phrase of the Dharma] that one hears, one would thus have heard before—and to be able to maintain all the Dharma that one has heard without forgetting, to be able to preach [the Dharma] to sentient beings without there being sentient beings, and without any distinction between self, sentient beings, and the Dharma being preached: this is called 'well versed'."

At that time there was in the assembly a Bodhisattva god named Pure Moon Store, who thought as follows: "The Buddha has taught that Ānanda was premier in being well-versed. But is Ānanda well-versed in the manner that has just been explained by Mañjuśrī?" When he had this thought, he asked Ānanda, "The Tathāgata has taught that you are premier in being well-versed. Are you well-versed in the manner just explained by Mañjuśrī?" Ānanda answered, "I am not well-versed in the manner explained by Mañjuśrī." Pure Moon Store Bodhisattva said, "Then why did the Tathāgata declare you to be premier in being well-versed?" Ānanda answered, "I am said to be premier among those disciples of the Buddha who have become emancipated upon following the sounds [of the Buddha's teachings]. This is not to say that I am premier in being well-versed among the Bodhisattvas, who have oceans of immeasurable wisdom, unequalled great sagacity, and unhindered discrimination. O god, it is likened to the brilliance of the sun and moon, by which the people of Jambudvīpa see the various forms and perceive their own activities. I am like this. However, with the brilliance of the wisdom of the Tathāgata one may maintain the Dharmas. I am powerless in this regard. You should understand that this is entirely the divine power of the Tathāgata."

The World-Honored One then praised Ānanda, saying, "Excellent, excellent! It is as you have spoken. You should understand 642a
that all the Dharmas which you maintain and recite are all [due to] the divine power of the Tathāgata."

Then the Buddha told Pure Moon Store, "The Dharmas maintained by Ānanda are extremely few; those he does not recite are immeasurable and infinite. O god, of the Dharmas I attained at my enlightenment (*lit.,* at my place of enlightenment, *bodhimaṇḍa*), I have preached not even a single hundred thousand hundred-millionth part. And of those that I have preached, Ānanda maintains not even a single hundred-thousand hundred-millionth part. O god, in just a single day and night, I preach the Dharma to all the Indra gods, Brahmā gods, world-protecting kings, gods, dragons, *yakṣa*s, *gandharva*s, *asura*s, *garuḍa*s, *kiṃnara*s, *mahoraga*s, and Bodhisattvas in all the worlds of the ten directions. With the power of my wisdom I compose verses and preach the Sūtras, stories, and parables, as well as [explanations of the] Perfections to be practiced by sentient beings. I also preach the Dharmas of the Śrāvaka and Pratyekabuddha Vehicles. The insurpassable Vehicle of the Buddhas encompasses the teaching of the Mahāyāna. I decry saṃsāra and praise Nirvāṇa. Even if all the sentient beings within Jambudvīpa were as well versed as Ānanda, they would be unable to maintain [all these Dharmas] for a hundred thousand eons. O god, because of this, you should understand that the Dharmas preached by the Tathāgata are innumerable and infinite, and that the portion maintained by Ānanda is extremely small."

At that point the god Pure Moon Store proffered to the Tathāgata a canopy made of a hundred thousand flowers of the seven precious things. The canopy immediately spread out throughout space, imparting a golden color onto all the sentient beings it covered. After proffering this canopy, he said, "Thus it is, World-Honored One. With this merit, I beseech you to grant all sentient beings the discrimination to preach the Dharma like you and to be able to maintain the Dharmas like Mañjuśrī, the Dharma prince." The Buddha then realized that this Bodhisattva god longed profoundly for the enlightenment of Buddhahood and conferred upon him a prediction of the achievement of insurpassable and perfect enlightenment, saying, "After four million four hundred thousand eons, this god will become a Buddha. His title will be Single Treasured Canopy and his land will be named Ornamented with All the Treasures."

When the Buddha said this, two hundred Bodhisattvas became discouraged, [thinking] "The Dharma of the Buddhas, the World-Honored Ones, is extremely profound, and insurpassable;

and perfect enlightenment is this difficult to achieve! We will not be able to complete the task! This is worse than if we had just entered Nirvāṇa as Pratyekabuddhas. Why? The Buddha has preached that if a Bodhisattva regresses he will become either a Pratyekabuddha or a Śrāvaka."

At that time Dharma Prince Mañjuśrī knew that these two hundred Bodhisattvas had become discouraged. Wishing to rekindle their intention to achieve insurpassable and perfect enlightenment, and also wishing to teach the gods, dragons, *yakṣa*s, *gandharva*s, *asura*s, *garuḍa*s, *kiṃnara*s, and *mahoraga*s in the assembly, he addressed the Buddha, saying, "World-Honored One, I remember an eon in the past named Luminous Brilliance, during which I entered Nir- 642b
vāṇa as a Pratyekabuddha in thirty-six billion lifetimes." Everyone in the assembly then became doubtful, [thinking that] "Someone who enters Nirvāṇa should not return to the succession of birth and death. How can Mañjuśrī say, 'World-Honored One, I remember an eon in the past named Luminous Brilliance, during which I entered Nirvāṇa as a Pratyekabuddha in thirty-six billion lifetimes.' How could this be?"

Śāriputra, taking up the Buddha's divine intent, then addressed the Buddha, saying, "World-Honored One, someone who enters Nirvāṇa should not return to the succession of birth and death. How could Mañjuśrī have entered Nirvāṇa and then return to be born?" The Buddha said, "You may ask Mañjuśrī. He will answer you himself." Śāriputra then asked Mañjuśrī, saying, "Anyone who enters Nirvāṇa should not return to the realms of existence. Why did you say 'World-Honored One, I remember an eon in the past named Luminous Brilliance, during which I entered Nirvāṇa as a Pratyekabuddha in thirty-six billion lifetimes?' What do you mean by this?"

Mañjuśrī said, "The Tathāgata is now [in the world]. He is the all-knowing one, the all-seeing one, the one who speaks the truth, the one who does not deceive, the one who cannot be deceived by the gods and people of this world. What I have said, the Buddha realizes to be true. If I have spoken incorrectly, then it would be to deceive the Buddha. Śāriputra, at that time in the Luminous Brilliance eon, there was a Buddha in the world named Puṣya, who entered Nirvāṇa after benefitting the gods and people of that world. The Dharma lasted for one hundred thousand years after the extinction of [Puṣya] Buddha. After the extinction of the Dharma, there were sentient beings there who had karmic connections [*lit.*, causes and conditions] to be saved as Pratyekabuddhas; but even if a hundred thousand hundred-million Buddhas had preached the Dharma to them they would not have believed it or accepted it—they could only achieve emancipation through [the impact of seeing] the body and deportment of a Pratyekabuddha. Since these sentient beings all longed for the enlightenment of Pratyekabuddhas, they would have had no opportunity [*lit.*, causes and conditions] to plant good roots if no Pratyekabuddha had appeared.

"In order to teach [those sentient beings], I then declared my body to be that of a Pratyekabuddha. Throughout all the countries, cities, towns, and villages, everyone knew that my body was that of a Pratyekabuddha, and I always manifested the physical form and deportment of a Pratyekabuddha. The sentient beings there had profound reverence, and they all made offerings of food and drink to me. After accepting [these offerings] and partaking of them, I considered how their [various] karmic dispositions [*lit.*, fundamental conditions] would make them responsive to hearing the Dharma. After preaching [the Dharma] to them I had my body fly up into the sky, like the king of the geese. Those sentient beings all became very happy at this, bowing their heads in obeisance to me with reverential minds and saying, 'We wish that in
642c the future we may all attain benefit in the Dharma such as you have!' Śāriputra, through these causes and conditions immeasurable and innumerable sentient beings planted good roots.

"When I realized that the people had developed feelings of laziness through offering me food [and were no longer striving for their own enlightenment], I announced to them that 'The time for my Nirvāṇa has arrived.' Upon hearing this, a hundred thousand sentient beings came to where I was, carrying flowers, incense, and oil. However, when I then entered the meditation of extinction [*nirodha-samāpatti*], because of my original vow I did not undergo final extinction, [even though] the sentient beings there said that my life had finished. In order to make offerings to me they cremated my body with fragrant wood, saying that I had really undergone extinction.

"I then proceeded to a great city in another country, where I proclaimed myself to be a Pratyekabuddha. The sentient beings there came with food and drink to make offerings to me, and I manifested the entry into Nirvāṇa there [as well]. They too said that I had undergone extinction, and they all came to make offerings and to cremate my body. Thus, O Śāriputra, did I spend a single small eon. For thirty-six billion lifetimes I took on the body of a Pratyekabuddha and manifested entry into Nirvāṇa. In those great cities I led three billion six hundred million sentient beings to salvation using the Vehicle of the Pratyekabuddha. Śāriputra, thus does a Bodhisattva use the Vehicle of the Pratyekabuddha to enter Nirvāṇa without undergoing permanent extinction."

When Mañjuśrī spoke these words, the six types of vibrations shook the trichiliocosm and a brilliant light illuminated everywhere. A trillion gods made offerings to Dharma Prince Mañjuśrī, raining heavenly flowers upon him and saying, "This is truly rare! We have today attained great benefit by seeing the Buddha, the World-Honored One, by seeing Mañjuśrī, the Dharma prince, and by hearing the preaching of the Śūraṅgama Samādhi. O World-Honored One, Dharma Prince Mañjuśrī has accomplished such an unprecedented Dharma! In what samādhi does he reside that he is able to manifest this unprecedented Dharma?"

The Buddha told the gods, "Mañjuśrī, the Dharma prince, is able to accomplish such rare and difficult feats because he resides in the Śūraṅgama Samādhi. When a Bodhisattva resides in this samādhi he performs the practice of faith for [sentient beings] yet does not follow any other faith. He also performs the practice of the Dharma and, with regard to the characteristic of the Dharma, neither regresses nor fails in the turning of the Wheel of the Dharma.

He also transforms himself into eight [different types of] persons and cultivates enlightenment during countless immeasurable eons on behalf of those beings [misled by] the eight heterodoxies [the opposites of the eightfold noble path]. He becomes a stream-enterer, but on behalf of sentient beings floating in the waters of saṃsāra he does not enter the absolute. He becomes a seldom-returner and manifests his body throughout the worlds. He becomes a once-returner and returns again to teach sentient beings. He becomes an Arhat and studies the Dharma of the Buddhas with constant energy. He becomes a Śrāvaka and preaches the Dharma with unhindered discrimination. He becomes a Pratyekabuddha, and in order to teach sentient beings having [appropriate] aptitudes [*lit.*, causes and conditions], he manifests entry into Nirvāṇa and
643a then, through the power of samādhi, returns to be born once again. O gods, Bodhisattvas who reside in this Śūraṅgama Samādhi are all pervasively able to practice the practices of the sages. In accordance with their stages they also preach the Dharma, although they do not reside therein."

When the gods heard the Buddha preach this doctrine, they all burst into tears, saying, "World-Honored One, if someone has already entered the rank of Śrāvaka or Pratyekabuddha, he [must] lose forever this Śūraṅgama Samādhi. However, O World-Honored One, even if someone has committed [any of] the five major transgressions, if he hears the preaching of this Śūraṅgama Samādhi, he will become an Arhat with his impurities exhausted and without entering into the absolute [i.e., extinction]. Why? Even if someone has committed [any of] the five major transgressions, after hearing this Śūraṅgama Samādhi and generating the intention to achieve insurpassable and perfect enlightenment, even though his original transgression would [ordinarily lead him to being] cast into the hells, by the good roots and the causes and conditions of hearing this samādhi he will instead achieve Buddhahood.

"World-Honored One, an Arhat with impurities exhausted is yet like a broken vessel, [because he is] permanently unable to receive this samādhi. World-Honored One, it is likened to an offering of ghee and honey, which is to be carried in various vessels by many people. One of those people may be careless and break the vessel [he is carrying], so that even though he arrives at the location where the ghee and honey is to be donated, it is of no benefit. Although he can satisfy himself, he cannot carry any back to give to others. Another person, who carries a vessel that remains complete and strong, is able to satisfy himself and carry the filled vessel to give to others. The ghee and honey stands for the correct Dharma of the Buddhas. Those who break the vessels they carry, who satisfy themselves without being able to carry any [ghee and honey] back to give to others, are the Śrāvakas and Pratyekabuddhas. Those carrying the whole vessels are the Bodhisattvas, who are able to satisfy themselves and also carry [the Dharma] back to all sentient beings."

At this time the two hundred Bodhisattvas [*lit.*, gods] who were about to regress from the intention to achieve insurpassable and perfect enlightenment, upon hearing the words of these gods, and upon hearing of the inconceivable power of the merit of Dharma Prince Mañjuśrī, experienced a profound intention to achieve insurpassable and perfect enlightenment. Dispensing with their previous inclinations to regress, they addressed the Buddha, saying, "We will never forsake this intention, even at the cost of personal injury or loss of life, and we will never forsake all sentient beings!

"World-Honored One, we only wish that we might hear the good roots and causes and conditions of this Śūraṅgama Samādhi and that we might attain the ten powers of the Bodhisattva. What are these ten? [They are] (1) the power of firm resolve in the intention to achieve enlightenment, (2) the power to attain profound faith in the inconceivable Dharma of the Buddhas, (3) the power to be well-versed in and not forget [the Dharma], (4) the power to travel tirelessly throughout saṃsāra, (5) the power of resolute great compassion for all sentient beings, (6) the power of resolute equanimity in charity, (7) the power of indestructibility in morality, (8) the power of resolute acceptance in forbearance, (9) the power of wisdom indestructible by demons, and (10) the power of joy of faith 643b in the profound Dharmas." The Buddha then told Resolute Mind Bodhisattva, "You should understand that any sentient beings who hear this Śūraṅgama Samādhi and are able to have faith and take joy in it, whether during my presence or after my extinction, will all attain these ten powers of the Bodhisattva."

At that time there was within the assembly a Bodhisattva named Mind of Name, who addressed the Buddha, saying, "World-Honored One, those who desire blessings should make offerings to the Buddhas. Those who desire wisdom should strive to be well-versed [in the Dharma]. Those who desire favorable rebirth should strive in morality. Those who desire great fortune should perform charity. Those who desire to attain a wondrous physical form should cultivate forbearance. Those who desire discrimination should honor teachers. Those who desire *dhāraṇīs* should transcend arrogance. Those who desire wisdom should cultivate correct mindfulness. Those who desire joy should dispense with all [that is] wrong. Those who desire to benefit sentient beings should generate the intention to achieve enlightenment. Those who desire wondrous sounds should cultivate true speech [honesty]. Those who desire merit should take pleasure in transcendence. Those who desire to seek the Dharma should associate with spiritual compatriots. Those who desire [to practice] seated meditation should separate themselves from disturbance. Those who desire understanding should cultivate meditation. Those who desire rebirth in the realms of Brahmā should cultivate the unlimited states of mind. Those who desire rebirth as gods or humans should cultivate the ten forms of good.

"[However], World-Honored One, those who desire good fortune, those who desire wisdom, those who desire favorable rebirth, those who desire great fortune, those who desire to attain a wondrous physical form, those who desire discrimination, those who desire *dhāraṇīs*, those who desire wisdom, those who desire joy, those who desire to benefit sentient beings, those who desire wondrous sounds, those who desire merit, those who desire to seek the Dharma, those who desire [to practice] seated meditation, those who desire understanding, those who desire rebirth in the realms of Brahmā, those who desire rebirth as gods or humans, those who desire Nirvāṇa, those who desire the attainment of all forms of merit: such persons should hear the Śūraṅgama Samādhi, remember it, recite it, preach it for others, and practice it as it has been preached."

[Mind of Name Bodhisattva then inquired,] "World-Honored One, how should the Bodhisattva cultivate this samādhi?"

The Buddha said, "Mind of Name, if a Bodhisattva is able to contemplate the dharmas as empty and unobstructed, with each moment of thought completely extinguished and transcending like and dislike, this is to cultivate this samādhi. Also, Mind of Name, one cannot study this samādhi by one approach alone. Why? In accordance with the activities [*hsing, saṃskāra*] of the minds and mental attributes [*hsin hsin-yu, citta-caitta*] of sentient beings, this samādhi has various practices. In accordance with the sensory realms [*ju, āyatana*] of the minds and mental attributes of sentient beings, this samādhi has various realms. In accordance with the entryways [*ju-men*] of the senses of sentient beings, this samādhi has various entryways. In accordance with the names and forms [*ming-se*] of sentient beings, Bodhisattvas who have attained this samādhi also manifest a variety of names and forms. To be able to understand thus is to cultivate this samādhi. In accordance with all the names and forms and physical characteristics of the Buddhas, Bodhisattvas who have attained this samādhi also manifest a variety of names and forms and physical charac- 643c
teristics. To be able to understand thus is to cultivate this samādhi. In accordance with [their] vision of all the Buddha lands, Bodhisattvas are also able to create such lands. This is to cultivate this samādhi."

Mind of Name Bodhisattva addressed the Buddha, "World-Honored One, it is extremely difficult to cultivate this samādhi." The Buddha told Mind of Name, "It is because of this that few Bodhisattvas reside in this samādhi, while many Bodhisattvas practice other samādhis."

Mind of Name Bodhisattva then addressed the Buddha, saying, "World-Honored One, Maitreya, who is now in the location of his penultimate birth [in the Tuṣita heaven] and who is to succeed you, must have attained insurpassable and perfect enlightenment. Has Maitreya attained the Śūraṅgama Samādhi?" The Buddha said, "Mind of Name, those Bodhisattvas who reside on the tenth stage, who are in the location of their penultimate birth [in the Tuṣita heaven], and who have attained the true rank of Buddhahood—every one of these [Bodhisattvas] has attained this Śūraṅgama Samādhi."

Maitreya Bodhisattva then manifested his divine power as follows: Mind of Name Bodhisattva and the rest of the assembly saw all the Jambudvīpa [continents in all the worlds of] the trichiliocosm. They saw Maitreya Bodhisattva in the center of each [Jambudvīpa], or in the heavens, or among humans, or as a monk, or as a householder, or as an attendant to the Buddha like Ānanda, or as one premier in wisdom like Śāriputra, or as one premier in supernormal powers like Maudgalyāyana, or as one premier in asceticism like Mahākāśyapa, or as one premier in preaching the Dharma like Pūrṇa, or as one premier in the precepts (or, esoteric practices) like Rāhula, or as one premier in maintaining the Vinaya like Upāli, or as one premier in the heavenly eye like Aniruddha, or as one premier in seated meditation like Revata. Thus did they see Maitreya in the form of those premier in all [aspects of the Dharma]. They saw him entering into the cities, towns, and villages begging, or preaching the Dharma, or in seated meditation. Everything that was seen by Mind of Name Bodhisattva and the great assembly was manifested by Maitreya Bodhisattva through the power of the supernormal abilities [achieved through] the Śūraṅgama Samādhi. After seeing all this, [Mind of Name Bodhisattva] addressed the Buddha in great joy, saying, "World-Honored One, it is likened to gold, which is not altered in nature even when refined! And all these Bodhisattvas can do likewise: in whatever they attempt, they are able to manifest the inconceivable Dharma-nature!"

Mind of Name Bodhisattva then addressed the Buddha, "World-Honored One, I suggest that if a Bodhisattva is able to penetrate the Śūraṅgama Samādhi, one should understand that he penetrates all religious practices. He penetrates the Vehicle of the Śrāvaka, the

Vehicle of the Pratyekabuddha, and the Great Vehicle (the Mahāyāna) of the Buddha." The Buddha said, "Thus it is, thus it is. It is as you have spoken. If a Bodhisattva is able to penetrate the Śūraṅgama Samādhi, he penetrates all religious practices."

At that time the elder Mahākāśyapa addressed the Buddha, 644a
"World-Honored One, I suggest that Dharma Prince Mañjuśrī has already been a Buddha in a past life. He has himself sat in the seat of enlightenment and turned the Wheel of the Dharma, and he has manifested entry into Parinirvāṇa to sentient beings." The Buddha said, "Thus it is, thus it is. It is as you have spoken, Kāśyapa. Long in the distant past, an immeasurable and innumerable [number of] inconceivable immeasurable eons ago, there was a Buddha who was called Paragon of the Dragons [as well as by the ten titles] Tathāgata, He Who Should Receive Offerings, Of Correct and Universal Understanding, Sufficient in Wise Practice, Well-Gone, He Who Understands the World, the Unsurpassed One, He Who Disciplines Humans, Teacher of Humans and Gods, and World-Honored Buddha. A thousand Buddha lands south of this world, there was a country called Universal Equivalence, which had neither mountains nor rivers, neither stones nor rocks, and neither hills nor dales. The land there was as flat as the palm of one's hand, and on it grew a soft grass, like that in Kaliṅga. When Paragon of the Dragons Buddha attained insurpassable and perfect enlightenment and first turned the Wheel of the Dharma in that world, he created an assembly of seven billion Bodhisattvas through his teaching. Eight billion people became Arhats, and ninety-six thousand people resided as Pratyekabuddhas [*lit.*, resided within the dharmas of the causes and conditions of Pratyekabuddhas]. Afterward, there were also an immeasurable number of Śrāvaka monks.

"Kāśyapa, the life span of Paragon of the Dragons Buddha was four million four hundred thousand years, during which time he saved humans and gods and then entered into Nirvāṇa. His physical relics were divided and distributed around the world, and there were erected thirty-six hundred-million stūpas, at which sentient beings made offerings to him. After that Buddha died, the Dharma remained for ten thousand years. When Paragon of the Dragons Buddha was about to enter Nirvāṇa, he conferred a prediction [of future enlightenment] on Brilliance of Wisdom Bodhisattva, saying, 'After I am gone, this Brilliance of Wisdom Bodhisattva will achieve insurpassable and perfect enlightenment. He will again be called Brilliance of Wisdom [Buddha].'

"Kāśyapa, could that Paragon of the Dragons Buddha of the world Universal Equivalence be anyone else? You must have no doubt! Why? It was none other than Mañjuśrī, the Dharma prince. Kāśyapa, you should now perceive the power of the Śūraṅgama Samādhi. It is by its power that the great Bodhisattvas manifest entry into the womb, are born, leave home, proceed to the Bodhi Tree, sit upon the seat of enlightenment, turn the wondrous Wheel of the Dharma, enter into Parinirvāṇa, and distribute their relics, without ever dispensing with the Dharma of the Bodhisattva and not entering final extinction at Parinirvāṇa."

The elder Mahākāśyapa then asked Mañjuśrī, "Are you able to perform such rare and difficult things to manifest for sentient beings?" Mañjuśrī said, "Kāśyapa, what do you mean? Who created this Mount Gṛdhrakūṭa? From whence did this world derive?" Kāśyapa replied, "Mañjuśrī, all the worlds are created out of foam, and they are derived from the causes and conditions of the incon-
644b ceivable karma of sentient beings." Mañjuśrī said, "All the dharmas also exist in dependence on the causes and conditions of inconceivable karma. I have no power to effect such things. Why? The dharmas are all based on causes and conditions. Since they are without any [ultimate] master, they may be created at will. If one understands this, such actions [as those described above] are not difficult. Kāśyapa, it would be difficult for someone who does not know of the Four Noble Truths to hear and believe in such things. Once one understands the Four Noble Truths and attains the supernormal powers, however, it is not difficult to hear and believe this."

At that time the World-Honored One sent his body up into space, to the height of seven *tāla* trees. Seated [in the air] in full lotus position, he emitted a refulgence from his body that illuminated throughout [all] the immeasurable worlds in the ten directions.

The entire assembly saw the immeasurable Buddhas of the ten directions and heard them from afar all preaching the Śūraṅgama Samādhi, without increase and without decrease. Those Buddhas of the ten directions also sent their bodies up into space, to the height of seven *tāla* trees. Seated [in the air] in full lotus position, they emitted refulgences from their bodies that illuminated throughout [all] the immeasurable worlds in the ten directions. The sentient beings in those [other worlds] also saw the body of Śākyamuni Buddha risen up in the air and sitting in full lotus position. Those assemblies [listening to the other Buddhas] then all took flowers and scattered them over Śākyamuni Buddha from afar, and everyone saw the collections of flowers combine in the air to form a flowered canopy. The Bodhisattvas, gods, dragons, *yakṣa*s, and *gandharva*s of this land all scattered flowers about over the other Buddhas; and everywhere flowered canopies were formed over the heads of the Buddhas.

Śākyamuni Buddha then reined in his supernormal ability of levitation, sat back down on his original seat, and told Resolute Mind, "This is the power of the supernormal abilities of the Tathāgata. The Tathāgata has manifested thus in order to increase the merit of sentient beings." When the Buddha manifested his supernormal abilities, eight thousand gods generated the intention to achieve insurpassable and perfect enlightenment. Also, as the preaching of the Śūraṅgama Samādhi was about to end, Resolute Mind and five hundred [other] Bodhisattvas attained the Śūraṅgama Samādhi. All of them had seen the divine power of the Buddhas of the ten directions, had attained the brilliance of wisdom in the profound Dharma of the Buddhas, resided on the tenth stage, and received the rank of Buddhas. [All] the worlds of the trichiliocosm [shook] with the six types of vibration, and a great refulgence was released that illuminated throughout [all] the worlds. A thousand ten-thousand dancers performed at once, and the gods rained various types of flowers down from the sky.

The Buddha then told Ānanda, "You should accept this Śūraṅgama Samādhi, recite it, and preach it extensively for people." Indra king Holding Mount Sumeru then said to the Buddha,

"World-Honored One, there is a limit to Ānanda's wisdom and memory. Since Śrāvakas follow the [teaching] of objectified sound [*t'a yin-sheng*, *lit.*, other sound], why do you confer this Dharma treasure of this samādhi on Ānanda?" Indra king Holding Mount
644c Sumeru then spoke in utter sincerity, "If I will truly be able to disseminate this precious samādhi now and in the future, then let all the trees here on Mount Gṛdhrakūṭa appear as Bodhi Trees, with a Bodhisattva beneath each one!" After Indra king Holding Mount Sumeru said this, all the trees were seen to be like Bodhi Trees, with a Bodhisattva visible beneath each and every tree. The Bodhi Trees all uttered the following words, "It is as Indra king Holding Mount Sumeru has said. Truly, this person must be able to disseminate this samādhi widely!"

At that time the gods, dragons, *yakṣa*s, and *gandharva*s addressed the Buddha in unison, saying, "World-Honored One, even if your lifetime were an entire eon, you should do nothing other [than preach the Śūraṅgama Samādhi]. Rather than preaching the Dharma for people using the Vehicle of the Śrāvakas—[even though you] preach the Dharma for each and every one so that you are always able to save sentient beings, just as at the time of your first turning of the Wheel of the Dharma—it would be better if you were to save people by preaching this Śūraṅgama Samādhi. Why? The [number of] sentient beings who would be saved by the Śrāvaka Vehicle is not even one part in a hundred of [those who would be saved by] the Bodhisattva Vehicle, [nor even] one part in a hundred thousand ten-thousand hundred-million, nor even [one part in] any number that could be described metaphorically. Thus does the Śūraṅgama Samādhi have immeasurable power to make all Bodhisattvas achieve [their goals] and become sufficient in the Dharma of the Buddhas."

Resolute Mind Bodhisattva then addressed the Buddha, saying, "World-Honored One, what will your life span truly be? When will you finally enter Nirvāṇa?" The Buddha said, "Resolute Mind, thirty-two thousand Buddha lands to the east of this world, there is a country named Ornamentation. There is a Buddha there who is called King of Autonomous Illumination and Ornamentation, [as well as by the ten titles] Tathāgata, He Who Should Receive Offerings, Of Correct and Universal Understanding, Sufficient in Wise Practice, Well-Gone, He Who Understands the World, the Unsurpassed One, He Who Disciplines Humans, Teacher of Humans and Gods, and World-Honored Buddha. He is now preaching the Dharma. Resolute Mind, my life span is the same as that of the Buddha King of Autonomous Illumination and Ornamentation." [Resolute Mind asked], "World-Honored One, what is the life span of this Buddha King of Autonomous Illumination and Ornamentation?" The Buddha told Resolute Mind, "You may go ask him yourself; he will answer you."

At that instant, the Buddha imparted his divine power unto Resolute Mind, who, through the power of the Śūraṅgama Samādhi and through the power of the supernormal abilities [deriving from] his own good roots, arrived in a single moment in that world [known as] Ornamentation. [Resolute Mind] placed his head on that Buddha's feet in worship, walked around him three times, then faced that Buddha and addressed him saying, "World-Honored One, what is your life span? When will you enter into Nirvāṇa?" That Buddha replied, saying, "My life span is the same as that of the Buddha Śākyamuni. If you wish to know, Resolute Mind, my life span is seven hundred immeasurable eons. The life span of the Buddha Śākyamuni 645a
is the same." Feeling great joy, Resolute Mind Bodhisattva then returned to this Sahā world. He addressed the Buddha, saying, "World-Honored One, that Buddha King of Autonomous Illumination and Ornamentation has a life span of seven hundred immeasurable eons. He told me your life span is the same as his."

At that time Ānanda arose from his seat, placed his robe over his right shoulder, held his palms together, and faced the Buddha. He addressed the Buddha, saying, "World-Honored One, according to my understanding of the doctrines you have preached, I suggest that it is you who, under a different name, benefit sentient beings in that Ornamentation world." The World-Honored One then praised Ānanda, saying, "Excellent, excellent. You are able to understand this by the power of the Buddhas. The body of that Buddha is my body; under a different name do I preach the Dharma and save sentient beings there. Ānanda, such autonomous power in the supernormal abilities is entirely the power of the Śūraṅgama Samādhi." The Buddha then told Resolute Mind Bodhisattva, "Resolute Mind, because of this, you should understand that my life span is seven hundred immeasurable eons, after which I will finally enter into Nirvāṇa."

Hearing that the life span of the Buddha was so inconceivably [long], everyone in the great assembly then experienced great joy and attained [an experience they] had never had before. They addressed the Buddha, saying, "World-Honored One, the divine power of the Buddhas is utterly unprecedented. All of their activities [*hsing*, practices] are inconceivable. You manifest such a brief life span in this [world], yet your real [life span] is seven hundred immeasurable eons. World-Honored One, we beseech you to allow all sentient beings to have inconceivably long life spans such as this!"

The World-Honored One then said to Resolute Mind once again, "The demons and demonic people within the countries, cities, towns, villages, and empty forests will not be able to gain mastery of this Śūraṅgama Samādhi." He also told Resolute Mind, "Any Dharma master who copies, recites, and explains this Śūraṅgama Samādhi should have no fear of humans or nonhumans but will attain twenty forms of inconceivable merit. What are these twenty forms of inconceivable merit? [They are]: inconceivable wisdom, inconceivable sagacity, inconceivable expedient means, inconceivable discrimination, inconceivable wisdom in the Dharma [*fa-ming*], inconceivable *dhāraṇīs*, inconceivable teachings [*fa-men*], inconceivable memory [of anything] at will, inconceivable power in the supernormal abilities, inconceivable discrimination of the words of sentient beings, inconceivable profound understanding of the longings of sentient beings, inconceivable attainment of vision of the Buddhas, inconceivable hearing of the Dharmas, inconceivable
645b able teaching of sentient beings, inconceivable autonomous mastery of samādhi, inconceivable creation of pure lands, inconceivable

most wondrous physical form, inconceivable autonomous mastery of merit, inconceivable cultivation of the Perfections, and inconceivable attainment of the Dharma of the Buddhas without regression. These are the twenty.

"Resolute Mind, anyone who copies or recites this Śūraṅgama Samādhi will attain these twenty forms of inconceivable merit. For this reason, Resolute Mind, anyone who wants to attain any of the benefits in this lifetime or the next should copy, recite, explain, and practice according to this Śūraṅgama Samādhi. Resolute Mind, if good men and women seeking the enlightenment of Buddhahood and engaged in the thousand ten-thousand eons of diligent cultivation of the Six Perfections hear this Śūraṅgama Samādhi, are able to accept it in faith without becoming discouraged, and are not upset or frightened by it, the blessings [accruing from this] will surpass those of anything else, and they will rapidly attain insurpassable and perfect enlightenment. How much more so for those who hear it, accept it, recite it, practice according to it, and explain it for people! Any Bodhisattva who wishes to hear the inconceivable Dharma of the Buddhas without being upset or frightened, who wishes to realize his own understanding of all the Dharmas of the Buddhas without being dependent on any other teaching, should cultivate and practice this samādhi. If you wish to hear a Dharma you have not heard before, to accept [the Dharma] in faith and without disagreement, you should hear this Śūraṅgama Samādhi."

When this *Śūraṇgama Samādhi Sūtra* was preached, innumerable sentient beings generated the intention to achieve insurpassable and perfect enlightenment! Twice that number [were able to] reside in the stage of non-regression, and twice that number attained the forbearance of the birthlessness of all dharmas! Eighteen thousand Bodhisattvas attained the Śūraṅgama Samādhi, and eighteen thousand monks and nuns, because they were not influenced by the dharmas, [achieved] the emancipation of the extinction of impurities [*lit.,* outflows] and attained Arhatship. Twenty-six thousand laymen and laywomen attained the purity of the Dharma eye with regard to the dharmas, and thirty *nayuta*s of gods attained the rank of sage.

After the Buddha had preached this Sūtra, Dharma Prince Mañjuśrī, Resolute Mind Bodhisattva, all the great Bodhisattvas, Śrāvakas, and great disciples, and all the gods, dragons, *gandharva*s, *asura*s, and people of the world, having heard what the Buddha had preached, joyously believed in and accepted it.

Here Ends the *Śūraṇgama Samādhi Sūtra*

Glossary

Ānanda: The name of the Buddha's cousin, close disciple, and personal attendant. He was renowned for his ability to recite all of the Buddha's sermons from memory.

Arhat: "One who is worthy" since he has attained a spiritual goal, usually the eradication of all passions. While Buddha is the highest rank on the Bodhisattva's path, Arhat is the highest on the Śrāvaka's. Being an Arhat is not considered good enough by the Mahayanists, who posit different virtues, such as charity, zeal, and compassion.

āyatana ("entrance"): The six *āyatana*s are the six sense organs: (1) the eye, (2) the ear, (3) the nose, (4) the tongue, (5) the body, and (6) the mind, which comprise all of the human sense organs. The twelve *āyatana*s are the six sense organs and their respective objects: (1) form, (2) sound, (3) odor, (4) flavor, (5) sensation, and (6) concepts. These comprise the entire epistemological world.

Bodhicitta: The initial desire, intent, or hope to attain enlightenment.

Bodhisattva: In the Mahāyāna, a selfless being with universal compassion who sees the universal emptiness of phenomena and is destined to become a Buddha.

dhāraṇī: A mystic phrase, spell, or incantation.

dhātu ("element," "world"): The three *dhātu*s are the three realms of samsara, namely the realms of desire, of (pure) form, and of non-form. The eighteen *dhātu*s are the twelve *āyatana*s (q.v.) plus their respective consciousnesses.

eightfold noble path: The eight aspects of practice aimed at attaining Nirvāṇa. The practitioner must develop: (1) right views, (2) right thought, (3) right speech, (4) right acts, (5) right livelihood, (6) right effort, (7) right mindfulness or recollection, and (8) right meditation. *See also* Four Noble Truths.

five major transgressions: Violations of the Five Precepts (q.v.).

Five Precepts: (1) Not to kill, (2) not to steal, (3) not to commit adultery, (4) not to speak falsely, and (5) not to drink intoxicants.

five modes of existence (five *gatis*): Sometimes translated as the five destinies of sentient beings. According to its own past karma (q.v.), a sentient being is born as a (1) god, (2) human being, (3) hungry ghost, (4) animal, or (5) hell being. All five kinds of beings, including gods, are within the samsaric world and are suffering. Only human beings have a chance to attain liberation from samsara; gods do not know that they are suffering, and in the other three states, suffering is too severe to handle.

Four Noble Truths: (1) Life is suffering. (2) The cause of suffering is desire. (3) There is a world without suffering called Nirvāṇa. (4) The means of attaining Nirvāṇa is the practice of the eightfold noble path (q.v.).

gandharva: A mythical being who is a celestial musician.

garuḍa: A mythical being that is half bird and half human.

karma ("action"): There are three kinds, of body, mouth, and mind. Karma is the cause of samsara, and its cessation is, therefore, the way to liberation from karmic existence. Avoiding the nihilistic extreme, Buddhist moralists maintain that the essence of action is volition (*cetanā*) and that the cause of suffering is passion (*kleśa*).

kiṃnara: A mythical being who is a heavenly vocal musician.

kṣatriya: The governmental or warrior caste in ancient India; a member of this caste.

mahoraga: A snake-like mythical being.

Mañjuśrī: The celestial Bodhisattva who represents the wisdom and realization of all Buddhas.

Māra: The demon who hinders Buddhist practice.

Nirvāṇa: The final goal of Buddhists; the extinction of all passions; the state of liberation.

non-returner (*anāgāmin*): One who, without coming back to this world, will appear in the world of the gods and from there will attain Nirvāṇa.

once-returner (*sakṛdāgāmin*): One who, after having returned once more to this world, will attain the end of suffering.

Pratyakabuddha: A solitary Buddha. A Buddha who has realized enlightenment alone and does not want to teach.

samādhi: A kind of meditation. A mental state in which the mind is focused on one point to the exclusion of all else. It aims at the cessation of karma (q.v). Nine kinds are often recognized: the four meditations (*dhyāna*) in the world of form, the four attainments (*samāpatti*) in the world of nonform, and finally the attainment of cessation (*nirodhasamāpatti*). The last, being beyond the three realms of samsara, is Nirvāṇa.

samsara: This world of suffering, which consists of the three *dhātus* (q.v.). The cause of samsara is karma (q.v.). The Four Noble Truths (q.v.) say that there is a world beyond samsara called Nirvāṇa.

Śāriputra: A disciple of Śākyamuni, known as the foremost of those possessed of great wisdom. The authors of the Prajñāpāramitā literature, who claimed that they had more profound wisdom, criticized Śāriputra.

Saṅgha: The Buddhist order, the monastic community. The fourfold Saṅgha consists of four assemblies: monks, nuns, laymen, and laywomen.

skandha ("aggregate"): The five aggregates, which comprise all phenomenal things, are (1) matter, (2) perception, (3) conception, (4) volition, and (5) consciousness.

stream-enterer (*srotāpanna*): One who has just entered the stream of noble disciples and who is sure to be delivered someday. He is no longer subject to rebirth in the lower modes of existence (hell beings, animals, and hungry ghosts).

Śrāvaka: A "hearer" of Śākyamuni's teaching. The Śrāvakas preserved the Buddha's words, observed monastic rules, and organized the teachings into three bodies of scriptures called *piṭaka*s. Mahayanists called the Śrāvaka tradition a deficient Vehicle (Hīnayāna).

three lower modes of existence: Hungry ghosts, animals, and hell beings. These beings cannot attain Nirvāṇa because their suffering is too severe to handle.

Three Vehicles: The Śrāvaka Vehicle, the Pratyekabuddha Vehicle, and the Bodhisattva Vehicle.

Triple Jewel: The Buddha, the Dharma, and the Saṅgha. The Buddha said that the truth (Dharma) is the only light (*dīpa*), but his followers worshipped him and believed their community to be of similar importance.

yakṣa: A kind of demi-god, a spirit of the woods and the earth, sometimes benevolent and sometimes not.

Index

A List of the Volumes of the BDK English Tripiṭaka (First Series)

Abbreviations

Ch.: Chinese
Skt.: Sanskrit
Jp.: Japanese
T.: Taishō Tripiṭaka

Vol. No.		Title	*T.* No.
1, 2	*Ch.*	Ch'ang-a-han-ching (長阿含經)	1
	Skt.	Dīrghāgama	
3–8	*Ch.*	Chung-a-han-ching (中阿含經)	26
	Skt.	Madhyamāgama	
9-I	*Ch.*	Ta-ch'eng-pên-shêng-hsin-ti-kuan-ching (大乘本生心地觀經)	159
9-II	*Ch.*	Fo-so-hsing-tsan (佛所行讃)	192
	Skt.	Buddhacarita	
10-I	*Ch.*	Tsa-pao-ts'ang-ching (雜寶藏經)	203
10-II	*Ch.*	Fa-chü-p'i-yü-ching (法句譬喩經)	211
11-I	*Ch.*	Hsiao-p'in-pan-jo-po-lo-mi-ching (小品般若波羅蜜經)	227
	Skt.	Aṣṭasāhasrikā-prajñāpāramitā-sūtra	
11-II	*Ch.*	Chin-kang-pan-jo-po-lo-mi-ching (金剛般若波羅蜜經)	235
	Skt.	Vajracchedikā-prajñāpāramitā-sūtra	

Vol. No.		Title	T. No.
11-III	*Ch.*	Jên-wang-pan-jo-po-lo-mi-ching (仁王般若波羅蜜經)	245
	Skt.	Kāruṇikārājā-prajñāpāramitā-sūtra (?)	
11-IV	*Ch.*	Pan-jo-po-lo-mi-to-hsing-ching (般若波羅蜜多心經)	251
	Skt.	Prajñāpāramitāhṛdaya-sūtra	
12-I	*Ch.*	Ta-lo-chin-kang-pu-k'ung-chên-shih-san-mo-yeh-ching (大樂金剛不空眞實三麼耶經)	243
	Skt.	Adhyardhaśatikā-prajñāpāramitā-sūtra	
12-II	*Ch.*	Wu-liang-shou-ching (無量壽經)	360
	Skt.	Sukhāvatīvyūha	
12-III	*Ch.*	Kuan-wu-liang-shou-fo-ching (觀無量壽佛經)	365
	Skt.	Amitāyurdhyāna-sūtra	
12-IV	*Ch.*	A-mi-t'o-ching (阿彌陀經)	366
	Skt.	Sukhāvatīvyūha	
12-V	*Ch.*	Ti-ts'ang-p'u-sa-pên-yüan-ching (地藏菩薩本願經)	412
	Skt.	Kṣitigarbhapraṇidhāna-sūtra (?)	
12-VI	*Ch.*	Yao-shih-liu-li-kuang-ju-lai-pên-yüan-kung-tê-ching (藥師琉璃光如來本願功德經)	450
	Skt.	Bhaiṣajyaguruvaiḍūryaprabhāsapūrva-praṇidhāna-viśeṣavistara	
12-VII	*Ch.*	Mi-lê-hsia-shêng-ch'êng-fo-ching (彌勒下生成佛經)	454
	Skt.	Maitreyavyākaraṇa (?)	
12-VIII	*Ch.*	Wên-shu-shih-li-wên-ching (文殊師利問經)	468
	Skt.	Mañjuśrīparipṛcchā (?)	
13-I	*Ch.*	Miao-fa-lien-hua-ching (妙法蓮華經)	262
	Skt.	Saddharmapuṇḍarīka-sūtra	
13-II	*Ch.*	Wu-liang-i-ching (無量義經)	276
13-III	*Ch.*	Kuan-p'u-hsien-p'u-sa-hsing-fa-ching (觀普賢菩薩行法經)	277
14–19	*Ch.*	Ta-fang-kuang-fo-hua-yen-ching (大方廣佛華嚴經)	278
	Skt.	Avataṃsaka-sūtra	

Vol. No.		Title	T. No.
20-I	*Ch.*	Shêng-man-shih-tzŭ-hou-i-ch'eng-ta-fang-pien-fang-kuang-ching (勝鬘師子吼一乘大方便方廣經)	353
	Skt.	Śrīmālādevīsiṃhanāda-sūtra	
20-II	*Ch.*	Chin-kuang-ming-tsui-shêng-wang-ching (金光明最勝王經)	665
	Skt.	Suvarṇaprabhāsa-sūtra	
21–24	*Ch.*	Ta-pan-nieh-p'an-ching (大般涅槃經)	374
	Skt.	Mahāparinirvāṇa-sūtra	
25-I	*Ch.*	Fo-ch'ui-pan-nieh-p'an-liao-shuo-chiao-chieh-ching (佛垂般涅槃略説教誡經)	389
25-II	*Ch.*	Pan-chou-san-mei-ching (般舟三昧經)	418
	Skt.	Pratyutpannabuddhasammukhāvasthitasamādhi-sūtra	
25-III	*Ch.*	Shou-lêng-yen-san-mei-ching (首楞嚴三昧經)	642
	Skt.	Śūraṅgamasamādhi-sūtra	
25-IV	*Ch.*	Chieh-shên-mi-ching (解深密經)	676
	Skt.	Saṃdhinirmocana-sūtra	
25-V	*Ch.*	Yü-lan-p'ên-ching (盂蘭盆經)	685
	Skt.	Ullambana-sūtra (?)	
25-VI	*Ch.*	Ssŭ-shih-êrh-chang-ching (四十二章經)	784
26-I	*Ch.*	Wei-mo-chieh-so-shuo-ching (維摩詰所説經)	475
	Skt.	Vimalakīrtinirdeśa-sūtra	
26-II	*Ch.*	Yüeh-shang-nü-ching (月上女經)	480
	Skt.	Candrottarādārikāparipṛcchā	
26-III	*Ch.*	Tso-ch'an-san-mei-ching (坐禪三昧經)	614
26-IV	*Ch.*	Ta-mo-to-lo-ch'an-ching (達磨多羅禪經)	618
	Skt.	Yogācārabhūmi-sūtra (?)	
27	*Ch.*	Yüeh-têng-san-mei-ching (月燈三昧經)	639
	Skt.	Samādhirājacandrapradīpa-sūtra	

Vol. No.		Title	*T.* No.
28	*Ch.*	Ju-lêng-ch'ieh-ching （入楞伽經）	671
	Skt.	Laṅkāvatāra-sūtra	
29-I	*Ch.*	Ta-fang-kuang-yüan-chio-hsiu-to-lo-liao-i-ching （大方廣圓覺修多羅了義經）	842
29-II	*Ch.*	Su-hsi-ti-chieh-lo-ching （蘇悉地羯羅經）	893
	Skt.	Susiddhikaramahātantrasādhanopāyika-paṭala	
29-III	*Ch.*	Mo-têng-ch'ieh-ching （摩登伽經）	1300
	Skt.	Mātaṅgī-sūtra (?)	
30-I	*Ch.*	Ta-p'i-lu-chê-na-chêng-fo-shên-pien-chia-ch'ih-ching （大毘盧遮那成佛神變加持經）	848
	Skt.	Mahāvairocanābhisambodhivikurvitādhiṣṭhāna-vaipulyasūtrendrarāja-nāma-dharmaparyāya	
30-II	*Ch.*	Ching-kang-ting-i-ch'ieh-ju-lai-chên-shih-shê-ta-ch'eng-hsien-chêng-ta-chiao-wang-ching （金剛頂一切如來眞實攝大乘現證大教王經）	865
	Skt.	Sarvatathāgatatattvasaṃgrahamahāyānābhi-samayamahākalparāja	
31–35	*Ch.*	Mo-ho-sêng-ch'i-lü （摩訶僧祇律）	1425
	Skt.	Mahāsāṃghika-vinaya (?)	
36–42	*Ch.*	Ssŭ-fên-lü （四分律）	1428
	Skt.	Dharmaguptaka-vinaya (?)	
43, 44	*Ch.*	Shan-chien-lü-p'i-p'o-sha （善見律毘婆沙）	1462
	Pāli	Samantapāsādikā	
45-I	*Ch.*	Fan-wang-ching （梵網經）	1484
	Skt.	Brahmajāla-sūtra (?)	
45-II	*Ch.*	Yu-p'o-sai-chieh-ching （優婆塞戒經）	1488
	Skt.	Upāsakaśīla-sūtra (?)	
46-I	*Ch.*	Miao-fa-lien-hua-ching-yu-po-t'i-shê （妙法蓮華經憂波提舍）	1519
	Skt.	Saddharmapuṇḍarīka-upadeśa	
46-II	*Ch.*	Fo-ti-ching-lun （佛地經論）	1530
	Skt.	Buddhabhūmisūtra-śāstra (?)	

Vol. No.		Title	T. No.
46-III	*Ch.*	Shê-ta-ch'eng-lun (攝大乘論)	1593
	Skt.	Mahāyānasaṃgraha	
47	*Ch.*	Shih-chu-p'i-p'o-sha-lun (十住毘婆沙論)	1521
	Skt.	Daśabhūmika-vibhāṣā (?)	
48, 49	*Ch.*	A-p'i-ta-mo-chü-shê-lun (阿毘達磨俱舍論)	1558
	Skt.	Abhidharmakośa-bhāṣya	
50–59	*Ch.*	Yü-ch'ieh-shih-ti-lun (瑜伽師地論)	1579
	Skt.	Yogācārabhūmi	
60-I	*Ch.*	Ch'êng-wei-shih-lun (成唯識論)	1585
	Skt.	Vijñaptimātratāsiddhi-śāstra (?)	
60-II	*Ch.*	Wei-shih-san-shih-lun-sung (唯識三十論頌)	1586
	Skt.	Triṃśikā	
60-III	*Ch.*	Wei-shih-êrh-shih-lun (唯識二十論)	1590
	Skt.	Viṃśatikā	
61-I	*Ch.*	Chung-lun (中論)	1564
	Skt.	Madhyamaka-śāstra	
61-II	*Ch.*	Pien-chung-pien-lun (辯中邊論)	1600
	Skt.	Madhyāntavibhāga	
61-III	*Ch.*	Ta-ch'eng-ch'êng-yeh-lun (大乘成業論)	1609
	Skt.	Karmasiddhiprakaraṇa	
61-IV	*Ch.*	Yin-ming-ju-chêng-li-lun (因明入正理論)	1630
	Skt.	Nyāyapraveśa	
61-V	*Ch.*	Chin-kang-chên-lun (金剛針論)	1642
	Skt.	Vajrasūcī	
61-VI	*Ch.*	Chang-so-chih-lun (彰所知論)	1645
62	*Ch.*	Ta-ch'eng-chuang-yen-ching-lun (大乘莊嚴經論)	1604
	Skt.	Mahāyānasūtrālaṃkāra	
63-I	*Ch.*	Chiu-ching-i-ch'eng-pao-hsing-lun (究竟一乘寶性論)	1611
	Skt.	Ratnagotravibhāgamahāyānottaratantra-śāstra	

Vol. No.		Title	*T.* No.
63-II	*Ch.*	P'u-t'i-hsing-ching (菩提行經)	1662
	Skt.	Bodhicaryāvatāra	
63-III	*Ch.*	Chin-kang-ting-yü-ch'ieh-chung-fa-a-nou-to-lo-san-miao-san-p'u-t'i-hsin-lun (金剛頂瑜伽中發阿耨多羅三藐三菩提心論)	1665
63-IV	*Ch.*	Ta-ch'eng-ch'i-hsin-lun (大乘起信論)	1666
	Skt.	Mahāyānaśraddhotpāda-śāstra (?)	
63-V	*Ch.*	Na-hsien-pi-ch'iu-ching (那先比丘經)	1670
	Pāli	Milindapañhā	
64	*Ch.*	Ta-ch'eng-chi-p'u-sa-hsüeh-lun (大乘集菩薩學論)	1636
	Skt.	Śikṣāsamuccaya	
65	*Ch.*	Shih-mo-ho-yen-lun (釋摩訶衍論)	1688
66-I	*Ch.*	Pan-jo-po-lo-mi-to-hsin-ching-yu-tsan (般若波羅蜜多心經幽贊)	1710
66-II	*Ch.*	Kuan-wu-liang-shou-fo-ching-shu (觀無量壽佛經疏)	1753
66-III	*Ch.*	San-lun-hsüan-i (三論玄義)	1852
66-IV	*Ch.*	Chao-lun (肇論)	1858
67, 68	*Ch.*	Miao-fa-lien-hua-ching-hsüan-i (妙法蓮華經玄義)	1716
69	*Ch.*	Ta-ch'eng-hsüan-lun (大乘玄論)	1853
70-I	*Ch.*	Hua-yen-i-ch'eng-chiao-i-fên-ch'i-chang (華嚴一乘教義分齊章)	1866
70-II	*Ch.*	Yüan-jên-lun (原人論)	1886
70-III	*Ch.*	Hsiu-hsi-chih-kuan-tso-ch'an-fa-yao (修習止觀坐禪法要)	1915
70-IV	*Ch.*	T'ien-t'ai-ssŭ-chiao-i (天台四教儀)	1931
71, 72	*Ch.*	Mo-ho-chih-kuan (摩訶止觀)	1911

Vol. No.		Title	*T*. No.
73-I	*Ch.*	Kuo-ch'ing-pai-lu (國清百録)	1934
73-II	*Ch.*	Liu-tsu-ta-shih-fa-pao-t'an-ching (六祖大師法寶壇經)	2008
73-III	*Ch.*	Huang-po-shan-tuan-chi-ch'an-shih-ch'uan-hsin-fa-yao (黄檗山斷際禪師傳心法要)	2012A
73-IV	*Ch.*	Yung-chia-chêng-tao-ko (永嘉證道歌)	2014
74-I	*Ch.*	Chên-chou-lin-chi-hui-chao-ch'an-shih-wu-lu (鎭州臨濟慧照禪師語録)	1985
74-II	*Ch.*	Wu-mên-kuan (無門關)	2005
74-III	*Ch.*	Hsin-hsin-ming (信心銘)	2010
74-IV	*Ch.*	Ch'ih-hsiu-pai-chang-ch'ing-kuei (勅修百丈清規)	2025
75	*Ch.*	Fo-kuo-yüan-wu-ch'an-shih-pi-yen-lu (佛果圜悟禪師碧巖録)	2003
76-I	*Ch.* *Skt.*	I-pu-tsung-lun-lun (異部宗輪論) Samayabhedoparacanacakra	2031
76-II	*Ch.* *Skt.*	A-yü-wang-ching (阿育王經) Aśokarāja-sūtra (?)	2043
76-III	*Ch.*	Ma-ming-p'u-sa-ch'uan (馬鳴菩薩傳)	2046
76-IV	*Ch.*	Lung-shu-p'u-sa-ch'uan (龍樹菩薩傳)	2047
76-V	*Ch.*	P'o-sou-p'an-tou-fa-shih-ch'uan (婆藪槃豆法師傳)	2049
76-VI	*Ch.*	Pi-ch'iu-ni-ch'uan (比丘尼傳)	2063
76-VII	*Ch.*	Kao-sêng-fa-hsien-ch'uan (高僧法顯傳)	2085
76-VIII	*Ch.*	Yu-fang-chi-ch'ao: T'ang-ta-ho-shang-tung-chêng-ch'uan (遊方記抄: 唐大和上東征傳)	2089-(7)
77	*Ch.*	Ta-t'ang-ta-tz'ŭ-ên-ssŭ-san-ts'ang-fa-shih-ch'uan (大唐大慈恩寺三藏法師傳)	2053

Vol. No.		Title	T. No.
78	*Ch.*	Kao-sêng-ch'uan（高僧傳）	2059
79	*Ch.*	Ta-t'ang-hsi-yü-chi（大唐西域記）	2087
80	*Ch.*	Hung-ming-chi（弘明集）	2102
81–92	*Ch.*	Fa-yüan-chu-lin（法苑珠林）	2122
93-I	*Ch.*	Nan-hai-chi-kuei-nei-fa-ch'uan（南海寄歸内法傳）	2125
93-II	*Ch.*	Fan-yü-tsa-ming（梵語雑名）	2135
94-I	*Jp.*	Shō-man-gyō-gi-sho（勝鬘經義疏）	2185
94-II	*Jp.*	Yui-ma-kyō-gi-sho（維摩經義疏）	2186
95	*Jp.*	Hok-ke-gi-sho（法華義疏）	2187
96-I	*Jp.*	Han-nya-shin-gyō-hi-ken（般若心經秘鍵）	2203
96-II	*Jp.*	Dao-jō-hos-sō-ken-jin-shō（大乘法相研神章）	2309
96-III	*Jp.*	Kan-jin-kaku-mu-shō（觀心覺夢鈔）	2312
97-I	*Jp.*	Ris-shū-kō-yō（律宗綱要）	2348
97-II	*Jp.*	Ten-dai-hok-ke-shū-gi-shū（天台法華宗義集）	2366
97-III	*Jp.*	Ken-kai-ron（顯戒論）	2376
97-IV	*Jp.*	San-ge-gaku-shō-shiki（山家學生式）	2377
98-I	*Jp.*	Hi-zō-hō-yaku（秘藏寶鑰）	2426
98-II	*Jp.*	Ben-ken-mitsu-ni-kyō-ron（辨顯密二教論）	2427
98-III	*Jp.*	Soku-shin-jō-butsu-gi（即身成佛義）	2428
98-IV	*Jp.*	Shō-ji-jis-sō-gi（聲字實相義）	2429
98-V	*Jp.*	Un-ji-gi（吽字義）	2430
98-VI	*Jp.*	Go-rin-ku-ji-myō-hi-mitsu-shaku（五輪九字明秘密釋）	2514

Vol. No.		Title	T. No.
98-VII	*Jp.*	Mitsu-gon-in-hotsu-ro-san-ge-mon (密嚴院發露懺悔文)	2527
98-VIII	*Jp.*	Kō-zen-go-koku-ron (興禪護國論)	2543
98-IX	*Jp.*	Fu-kan-za-zen-gi (普勸坐禪儀)	2580
99–103	*Jp.*	Shō-bō-gen-zō (正法眼藏)	2582
104-I	*Jp.*	Za-zen-yō-jin-ki (坐禪用心記)	2586
104-II	*Jp.*	Sen-chaku-hon-gan-nen-butsu-shū (選擇本願念佛集)	2608
104-III	*Jp.*	Ris-shō-an-koku-ron (立正安國論)	2688
104-IV	*Jp.*	Kai-moku-shō (開目抄)	2689
104-V	*Jp.*	Kan-jin-hon-zon-shō (觀心本尊抄)	2692
104-VI	*Ch.*	Fu-mu-ên-chung-ching (父母恩重經)	2887
105-I	*Jp.*	Ken-jō-do-shin-jitsu-kyō-gyō-shō-mon-rui (顯淨土眞實教行証文類)	2646
105-II	*Jp.*	Tan-ni-shō (歎異抄)	2661
106-I	*Jp.*	Ren-nyo-shō-nin-o-fumi (蓮如上人御文)	2668
106-II	*Jp.*	Ō-jō-yō-shū (往生要集)	2682
107-I	*Jp.*	Has-shū-kō-yō (八宗綱要)	蔵外
107-II	*Jp.*	San-gō-shī-ki (三教指帰)	蔵外
107-III	*Jp.*	Map-pō-tō-myō-ki (末法燈明記)	蔵外
107-IV	*Jp.*	Jū-shichi-jō-ken-pō (十七條憲法)	蔵外